Staying or Leaving the Course

Staying or Leaving the Course

*Non-Completion and Retention of
Mature Students in Further and
Higher Education*

Veronica McGivney

promoting adult learning

Published by the
National Institute of Adult Continuing Education
(England and Wales)
Renaissance House, 20 Princess Road West, Leicester LE1 6TP

Company registration no. 2603322
Charity registration no. 1002775

First published 1996
Reprinted 2001, 2002
This second edition published 2003

niace
promoting adult learning

NIACE has a broad remit to promote lifelong learning opportunities for
adults. NIACE works to develop increased participation in education and
training, particularly for those who do not have easy access because of
barriers of class, gender, age, race, language and culture, learning
difficulties and disabilities, or insufficient financial resources.

For a full catalogue of NIACE's publications, please visit
http://www.niace.org.uk/publications

Cataloguing in Publications Data
A CIP record for this title is available from the British Library

ISBN 1 86201 175 3

Cover design by: Hobo Design Associates, Leicester
Designed and typeset by: Newgen Imaging Systems (P) Ltd., Chennai, India
Printed and bound in Great Britain by Antony Rowe Ltd., Chippenham, Wilts

Contents

Foreword to the Second Edition

This is the second edition of Staying or Leaving the Course which was based on a study conducted in the mid-1990s. Although the policy context has changed considerably since then, many of the issues explored in the study have not. For this reason, except for some minor amendments, the original text remains substantially the same as in the first edition.

Since 1996 when *Staying or Leaving the Course* was published, there have been a number of developments which have significantly changed the landscape of post-compulsory education and training. The New Labour Government elected in 1997 introduced significant structural and funding changes in the adult, further and higher education sectors. These notably included the replacement of the Further Education Funding Council (FEFC) and the Training and Enterprise Councils (TECs) with the Learning and Skills Council (LSC) which now has overall responsibility for post-16 education and training outside the higher education sector; the introduction of tuition fees for students in higher education, and the introduction of Educational Maintenance Allowances (EMAs) for young people staying in education after the age of 16. The new Government also launched a succession of other initiatives designed to improve the quality of learning opportunities and to make education provision more accessible to the social groups least represented in the programmes offered in the different education sectors.

Since the report of the National Committee of Inquiry into Higher Education (Dearing, 1997) there has been particular concern with widening the social mix of students entering *higher* education. This has now taken on a specific focus – the achievement of the Government's target of an HE participation rate of at least 50 per cent among young people under the age of 30 by 2010, in pursuit of which a set of proposals were put forward in the document *Partnerships for Progression*, produced by the Higher Education Funding Council for England (HEFCE) and the LSC (HEFCE/LSC, 2002).

Quality Assurance

The focus on quality assurance in the post-compulsory system has, if anything, grown stronger since 1997, and this has included an increasing concern with student retention and non-completion:

> '*"Wastage" in any system becomes a focus of interest when efficiency gains are required. (...) Prior to 1997, interest in higher education non-completion (or the obverse - retention) was minimal.' (Longden, 2002: 17).*

The situation is now the opposite. Annual retention and achievement targets were set for colleges from 1998–99, based on benchmarking data introduced in 1997. In 1999, HEFCE published indicators for HEIs setting out student continuation and projected achievement rates. In his annual letter to the Chair of HEFCE in 2000, the then Secretary of State for Education and Employment, David Blunkett, said that he expected the Council to 'bear down on the rate of "drop-out"'. In 2001, both the Parliamentary Select Committee on Education and Employment and the National Audit Office examined the issues of non-completion and retention in HE.

Despite this acceleration of interest, the actual rate of attrition does not seem to have changed significantly since 1997 in either further or higher education. The National Audit Office (2001) states that 15 per cent of students in FE colleges are failing to complete their courses and the Parliamentary Select Committee on Education and Employment (2001) estimates that about one in six students who enter HE leave without completing their degree. These figures are not dissimilar to those obtained before 1997. Britain's completion rates also still compare very favourably with those in other countries. However, there is a widespread perception that the increasing admission of 'non-traditional' students to higher education is leading to higher non-completion rates: 'Since the move towards mass higher education in the 1990s, levels of concern about rates of student retention and non-completion in HE have been on the rise' (Longden, 2002). Some maintain that overall standards are being jeopardised while others are more concerned with the need to support the new groups of students who are entering the system: 'Notwithstanding progress on recruitment, institutions should focus on retaining students, particularly those from disadvantaged backgrounds'. (Blunkett, 2000: para 11).

There is also increasing worry about the financial implications of non-completion. In a HEFCE-commissioned study, Yorke *et al.* (1997) estimated the cost of non-completion to be of the order of £91 million per year.

Plus ça Change...

Thus, although retention rates have remained relatively steady over the last six years, there is a strong policy momentum to improve them. A number of the recent reports on the subject have itemised the kinds of measures that might contribute to the achievement of this aim. Many of these are substantially the same as the measures discussed in the final sections of *Staying or Leaving the Course*. Most of the reports and studies on non-completion since 1997 also report the same complex interplay of personal, institutional and course-related reasons for non- completion that are explored in *Staying or Leaving the Course*. The main change is that in HE, the issues of student financial support and debt have since become critical, together with the related issue of students taking on part-time work which can interfere with achievement and completion rates.

Many of the other issues explored in the book also remain essentially unchanged, for example:

- The problem of definition: 'There are no nationally or internationally agreed definitions of non-completion and a wide range of possible constructions and interpretations exist' (Parliamentary Select Committee on Education and Employment, 2001).
- The failure of some institutions to adapt to a more diverse body of students: 'The evidence shows there are unacceptable variations in the rate of "drop out" which appear to be linked more to the culture and workings of the institution than to the background or nature of the students recruited' (Blunkett, 2000).
- Inadequate provision of information to and preparation of students before they engage in higher-level study at an FE or HE institution. The UCAS (2002) report found that few non-traditional HE students had managed to obtain detailed information on courses or to have some preparatory experience of HE.
- The need for financial support. The introduction of Educational Maintenance Grants (EMAs) has made a difference to staying on rates among some groups of young people. Research by the Institute of Employment Studies also found that financial support is particularly important for learners taking lower-level qualifications:

'It seems that financial support has a greater effect on those taking lower-level qualification where drop-out rates are highest. Drop-out rates decline from 23.7% for 'other' qualifications and 21.9% at Level 1, to only 12.5% at Level 3. Students studying for 'other' qualifications without support were 90% more likely than those with learner support funds to withdraw. For those at Levels 1, 2 and 3,

*the respective differences are 66.3%, 18.6% and 11.9%. It
suggests that financial support is likely to be particularly
significant for the widening participation and basic skills
initiatives.' (Reported in Fletcher, 2002)*

In HE it is now conceded that the changes in student
funding have had a detrimental impact on the widening
participation agenda.

* The difficulty of identifying and advising those students
  most at risk of non-completion: 'Less than half of the non-
  completers involved in the qualitative research had talked
  over their decision with staff' (NAO, 2002).

As was beginning to happen when *Staying or Leaving the
Course* was written, concern about non-completion has been
increasing at a time when resources in HE have been diminishing.
This has led to decreasing levels of teaching and pastoral support
for students. Worries about this have surfaced in recent reports and
other publications on non-completion:

*'Staff:student ratios declined from an average of 1:9 in 1980 to
1:17 in 1997 (if the funding for research that is included in the
average unit of funding is excluded, the staff: student ratio for
teaching worsens to approximately 1:23. In the less-well-
funded institutions the actual ratios are even less impressive,
During this time, class sizes grew ands opportunities for one to
one contact with staff diminished.' (The Parliamentary Select
Committee on Education and Employment, 2001: para 4)*

*'Strong evidence exists that the unit of funding per student FTE
has been reducing year on year.' (Longden, 2002: 14)*

The impact of diminishing resources may have been exacerbated by the Research Assessment Exercise (RAE) in higher education. With its financial implications for institutions, this has
inevitably been focusing minds more on research output than on
quality teaching and support for students.

In recent debates about the future funding of HE, concerns
have also been expressed that the differential institutional funding
desired in some quarters could lead to a division of institutions into
high-status research institutions inaccessible to less affluent students and lower-status, widening participation institutions.

In some ways, therefore, the widening participation and quality agendas are pulling against each other and the latter is to a certain extent militating against the achievement of higher retention

rates. Unless they have the resources to provide high staff:student ratios and good support procedures, institutions with a commitment to widening access among socio-economically disadvantaged groups are at higher risk of having higher non-completion rates than those institutions which still recruit traditional young, middle-class, academically qualified students. There is a temptation to do this as institutions can be penalised financially if students withdraw from courses before completion. However, the highest costs, emotional as well as financial, may be incurred by the students themselves, especially those who have taken a real leap into the unknown by embarking on a non-traditional and uncertain educational path.

Although the educational context has changed, therefore, many of the issues explored in *Staying or Leaving the Course* have not, and until they are addressed, the policy concern with reducing non-completion rates may amount to little more than whistling in the wind.

Veronica McGivney

References

Blunkett, D. (2000) '*Annual letter to the Chair of HEFCE*.'

Dearing, R. (1997) 'Higher Education in the Learning Society: Report of the National Committee of Enquiry into Higher Education', London: HMSO.

Dodgson, R. (2002) 'Widening participation and student retention in the NE of England.' *Update on Inclusion*, 4.

Fletcher, M. (2002) *Learning and Skills Research*, Summer, London: LSDA, p.38.

HEFCE/LSC (2002) *Partnerships for Progression*, London: HEFCE/ LSC.

Longden, B. (2000) 'Retention rates – renewed interest but whose interest is being served?', *Research Papers in Education*, 17(1), 3–29.

The National Audit Office (2001) '*Improving Student Performance: How English Further Education Colleges Can Improve Student Retention and Achievement*.' Report by the Comptroller and Auditor General.

The National Audit Office (2002) *Improving Student Achievement in English Higher Education*. Report by the Comptroller and Auditor General.

The Parliamentary Select Committee on Education and Employment (2001) *6th Report*.

UCAS (2002) *Paving the Way*, Cheltenham: UCAS.

Yorke, M. *et al.* (1997) *Undergraduate Non-completion in HE in England*, a HEFCE-commissioned report, London: HEFCE.

Preface

This report is the outcome of a short research project, funded by the former Employment Department, involving a study of the attendance and withdrawal patterns of mature students in further and higher education. It was conducted between March and September 1995. The aims of the project were:

- to examine the extent of and reasons for mature student delayed completion and withdrawal from adult, further and higher education courses and programmes of study
- to identify factors leading to withdrawal from courses and programmes of study
- to identify student groups and subject areas particularly susceptible to high withdrawal rates
- to identify measures that might improve retention and completion rates
- to examine the implications of changing patterns of participation for institutions and funding bodies.

Its objectives were:

- to examine existing data and research studies
- to obtain recent data from a sample of institutions
- to obtain further institutional perspectives on the nature of and reasons for delayed completion and withdrawal among mature students.

Methods

The project adopted a largely qualitative approach, involving:

- a literature search
- a consultation meeting with representatives from adult, further and higher education
- a postal survey of a small sample of further and higher education institutions (Appendix 1)
- contact with a sample of Access Validating Agencies
- correspondence and telephone contact with researchers and practitioners with a known interest in retention and non-completion issues.

A consultation meeting with 18 representatives from different sectors was held in March 1995 and interim findings were presented

Acknowledgements

NIACE would like to thank the Employment Department (now part of the Department for Education and Employment) for supporting this project.

I should also like to thank most sincerely the many people who assisted the project by attending the consultation meeting, sending data and research reports, completing questionnaires and discussing and advising on relevant issues. Some institutions returned questionnaires without including a contact name, and to them also I am grateful.

Kate Atkinson (Barnsley College); Mark Atlay (Bedfordshire Access Consortium); Malcolm Barry (Goldsmiths College); Geoff Bateson (Birmingham LEA); Gill Beeston (The Essex Access Consortium); Roseanne Benn (University of Exeter); Rita Bond (National Extension College); Lorraine Brown (University of Northumbria at Newcastle); Wyngrove Brown (Pontypridd College); David Burtenshaw (University of Portsmouth); Elaine Capizzi (City University); Malcolm Charnley (Swansea College); Timothy Chilcott (West Sussex Institute of Higher Education); Roger Clewett (Gwent Tertiary College, Newport Campus); Coleg Powys; Nancy Dando (Llandrillo College); Christine Daniels (University of Wales, Cardiff); Jay Derrick (City and Islington College); Sian Dodderidge (City of Wakefield Metropolitan District Council); David Finch (Coleg Afan College); Dr W.T. Green (NORAC); Vicki Goodwin (The Open University); Caroline Harvey (Norton Radstock College); Amanda Hayes (Kensington and Chelsea College); Phil Hobbs (Exeter College); David Istance (University of Wales, Swansea); Geoff Jones (Aberdare College); Janet Jones (Gwent Tertiary College, Ebbw Vale Campus); Philip Jones (HEQC); Phoebe Lambert (Liverpool John Moores University); Ruth Lawford (Tees-Wear Access Federation); Georgina Llewellyn (Bangor Normal College); Mid Glamorgan Technical College; Rebecca Moore (Sheffield Hallam University); Annabel Morley (Cambridge Access Validating Agency); Lyn Paton (Lancaster University/Open College of the North West); Sue Pedder (London Open College Federation); Jim Pye (Oxford Brookes University); Sarah Reid (University of Wales, Swansea); Anna Reisenberger (FEDA); Pat Rickwood (Open University, West Midlands Region); Ian Salmon (University of Wales, Aberystwyth); John Sanders (Merseyside Open College Federation); Derek Sarath

(Wirral Metropolitan College); Elaine Seer (S.E. Wales Access Consortium AVA); Steve Smith (Yale College); John Storan (South Bank University); Carole Stott (University of Warwick); Christine Thomas (University of Bradford); Alastair Tranter (Cheshire County Council Education Services); Cal Weatherald (Sheffield Hallam University); Claire Whatnall (N.E. Midlands Access Partnership AVA); Diane Williams (Gwent Tertiary College, Ebbw Vale Campus); Michael Williams (Carmarthenshire College of Technology and Arts); Sarah Williams (University of Coventry); David Wilson (Northamptonshire LEA); Paula Whittle (Basildon College).

I should also like to thank Averil Coutinho and Helen Balmforth for their invaluable help with organising and administering the project, Carolyn Winkless for helping to supply documentary evidence, Anne Poole for contacting institutions in Wales, and Trevor Seymour for his patient help and advice on computer problems.

Chapter 1

The Context

Changes in the structure and funding of post-compulsory education and in the composition of the student body have focused attention on retention and non-completion rates. Institutions are now required to monitor retention rates and collect and record student data more carefully and in more detail than in the past. However, concerns about funding and reputation have made non-completion a sensitive issue and institutions are not always keen to publicise their rates.

Since the beginning of the 1990s, changes in economic patterns have combined with changes in education policy and structures to create a new landscape for adult learners.[1] In the last few years, funding constraints and policy changes have led to a strong shift towards certificated provision for adults; further education colleges have been incorporated and now receive public funding from the Further Education Funding Councils; higher education has become a unified system with funding in the hands of the Higher Education Funding Councils and quality currently the responsibility of the Higher Education Quality Council.

In both sectors, the traditional student body has changed considerably over the last 10 to 15 years, a trend encouraged by increasing flexibility in entry requirements, course structures, learning modes and assessment methods. FEFC funding of the tranche of courses which fall under Schedule 2 has assisted adult access to further education, as has the rapid development of Access courses, modularisation, and open and flexible learning. Higher education has also become more accessible to adults through more flexible entry requirements, Access arrangements, assessment of prior learning and experience, credit accumulation and transfer schemes (CATS), modularisation, and distance and open learning approaches. In 1994, approximately 80 per cent of universities and colleges had or were committed to developing modular arrangements; nearly 85 per cent had or planned to introduce a CAT scheme; over 65 per cent had or planned to adopt a two-semester structure; and 70 per cent allowed credit for work-based and other forms of experiential learning

(Robertson, 1994). There are now:

> '*a growing number of universities within which students may obtain a learning experience based on wider choice, mobility and an achievement-led curriculum organised by modules, outcomes and credits*' *(Robertson, 1994: 10)*.

Partnerships between further and higher education institutions have also assisted adult access. In 1993, there were 10,000 students registered on bilateral 'franchised' programmes (McNair, 1993) and, by 1995, almost 20 per cent of further education colleges were offering degree or sub-degree courses supported by the HEFC (*Times Higher*, 20 January 1995). Other 'bridging' arrangements such as open college networks and access courses have also created progression routes for adults and have particularly facilitated the access of women, black learners and (albeit to a lesser extent) people from lower socio-economic groups. Davies (1995) estimates that there were about 13,000 Access entrants to higher education in 1993.

Other factors have also contributed to changes in the student population. Changing economic conditions have been encouraging adults to seek education and training, while pressures to become more competitive and meet growth targets have encouraged the further and higher education sectors to recruit more mature students. In the case of higher education, expansion rapidly exceeded government expectations and student numbers were capped in 1993. Further education, however, is required to continue to expand, a decision which may have been influenced by 'concern about the need for technical and intermediate skills, and perceptions of graduate oversupply' (McNair, 1993).

Mature Student Numbers and Profile

A combination of concurrent factors and developments have therefore resulted in a sharp increase in the numbers of adult learners entering further and higher education. In both sectors, adults now constitute a sizeable proportion of the total student population.

In further education, the number, in Full-Time Equivalent (FTE) terms, of adult students (usually defined as those over 19 as opposed to the traditional 16–19-year-old student body) rose by over 17 per cent from 1989/90 to 1993/94 (DFE, 1995) (Figures 1 and 2). In 1991, 51 per cent of enrolments were by students over 25. According to the FEFCE Chief Inspector's Report 1994–95, about three-quarters of students in the sector are adults, most of whom attend on a part-time basis.

Further education, by virtue of its work with employers, has always had a proportion of mature students. In higher education,

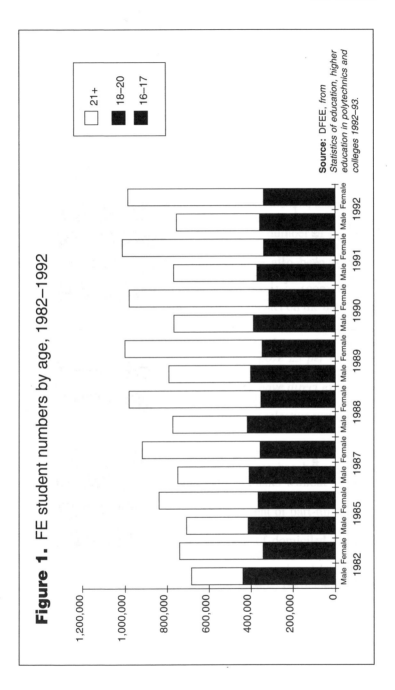

Figure 1. FE student numbers by age, 1982–1992

Legend:
- □ 21+
- ■ 18–20
- ■ 16–17

Source: DFEE, *from Statistics of education, higher education in polytechnics and colleges 1992–93.*

Financial imperatives

Funding for post-compulsory education and training has become increasingly linked to evidence of student attendance, completion and outcomes. In the training sector, Training and Enterprise Councils are increasingly contracting on an outcome-related funding basis, while in further and higher education, student numbers and retention rates are now used in the distribution formulae used by the UK funding councils.

At the same time, official concerns with quality, effectiveness and accountability have led to calls for more careful monitoring of student progress. In 1993, the Audit Commission recommended tracking of completion and non-completion rates in further education and the inclusion of non-completion rates for all courses in published results. It also proposed that funding structures 'should not encourage indiscriminate recruitment to courses' (Audit Commission, 1993).

Of the six performance indicators applied to colleges from the 1994/95 college year, three specifically relate to student numbers, retention and outcomes:

- students' enrolment trends as an indicator of college responsiveness
- student continuation as an indicator of programme effectiveness
- student achievements.

As pointed out by the former Further Education Unit (1993), 'in a demand and achievement led system, failure by an individual to attend, "achieve" or "complete" means non-payment for the college.'

Growth targets

A further requirement has been for colleges to meet a 28 per cent growth target within four years in order to achieve full core funding (subsequently scaled down for the year 1996–7). If they fail to expand, they may lose some of their core funding for the following year. This is creating some difficulty for individual institutions and according to one report (*Times Higher*, 17 March 1995), some have already incurred financial penalties because of failure to meet targets for the academic year. Moreover, a number of colleges have fully exploited the available pool of school leavers at a time when there is increasing competition from 'predatory sixth forms' (*ibid.*) and when full-time participation by the 16-plus cohort has peaked (Utley, 1995). Many colleges are therefore seeking to recruit more adult learners in order to meet the expansion targets. According to one respondent to this enquiry:

> *'There's a lot of competition from Sixth Form Colleges for our traditional students and our college has recognised that our growth area is in the adult market.'*

However, a survey conducted in 1994 suggested that many colleges are not yet adept at recruiting adults:

> *'Thousands of adults seeking a return to education this Summer were discouraged after finding college doors closed for holidays throughout August. Many colleges which did offer enrolments left ill-trained or demotivated staff in charge. Others offered brochures or telephone information which, the potential recruits said, seemed designed to dissuade them.*
>
> *The evidence belies the claims of many colleges to have open-all-year policies. Colleges in rural areas were the greatest offenders, the survey of one in four of all FE and tertiary colleges in England suggests. They believed sincerely but incorrectly that there was insufficient demand' (Times Educational Supplement, 9 September 1994).*

There are also signs that it is not as easy as it was a few years ago to tap 'ready-made' adult markets. On the one hand there has been a slump in employer demand for day release and block courses and on the other, consolidation of numbers in higher education has put a question mark over the further development of partnerships with higher education to assist progression of 'non-standard' entry students. As Bargh *et al.* (1994) have pointed out, any freezing of opportunities for non-standard students will cause serious difficulties for those colleges which have invested heavily in progression routes into higher education.

Thus it is now widely believed that colleges will need to recruit more part-time students in order to achieve their target numbers:

> *'Colleges that missed targets last year did so partly because of failures in part-time adult recruitment. An analysis of 1993 recruitments by the Further Education Funding Council last term showed that while the 8 per cent target for increased recruitment of full-time 16- to 19-year-olds was comfortably reached, adult numbers rose by only 4 per cent. The FEFC Chief Executive said: "If FE is to achieve these targets, it will not only have to keep up full-time enrolments, but succeed more with part-timers" ' (Times Educational Supplement, 9 September 1994).*

The Further Education Funding Council translates student expansion targets into units and this makes it possible for extra units to be gained by the same number of students *provided that* retention, completion and achievement rates improve. Colleges are required to notify the FEFC of the number of students who have enrolled and are still attending on three census dates during the year – at the beginning of November, February and May. These figures form the basis for calculating a college's funding allocation for the next year and any adjustments required for the current year. The students enrolled in the different course categories (full-time and short intensive; part-time day; part-time evening) will only be funded if they are actively attending on each census date (i.e. have enrolled and, where appropriate, paid a fee which covers the current term; have not withdrawn or are on a programme that has not come to an end).

These requirements have focused minds on the consequences of high withdrawal rates and the need to improve student retention, as illustrated by comments from several of the colleges contacted during the project:

> *'The new funding regime has certainly raised the profile of student retention.'*

> *'Funding Council decisions about definitions of withdrawal have concentrated our attention on the support mechanisms for part-time students.'*

Higher education institutions have also been forced to confront issues relating to retention and non-completion. In this sector, the policy decision to consolidate student numbers and freeze participation rates has led to cuts in first-year intakes averaging 3.5 per cent. A maximum aggregate student number (MASN) has been set for each institution, taking into account institutional growth patterns between 1992/93. The MASN includes all home and European Union students whose fees are paid by government and local government and continuing students. Institutions which exceed or underachieve their MASN face financial penalties. Any institution that exceeds its MASN by more than 1 per cent will lose the residual fee income it gains through over-recruitment.

The new system has made it difficult for some institutions to plan for the exact number of required students. Under the unified admission system (UCAS) that has been in place since 1993, applicants can make a maximum of eight choices but hold only two offers. It has been pointed out that this has upset existing assumptions about how many offers need to be made to fill a specified number of places (Payne and Stoman, 1995). Secondly, Higher Education Funding Council (HEFC) methodology requires universities to count all students who are enrolled as of the second of November or later, and to predict the number who will withdraw or fail to complete the year. The net number of students in the November returns, after subtraction of predicted withdrawals, is used to calculate the average unit of council funding (AUCF) in each academic subject category. This calculation is used to determine an institution's ability to acquire additional core funding. However, it is not always easy to forecast how many students are likely to continue, and in recent years early withdrawal rates have apparently become increasingly unpredictable:

'Although most institutions are able to make reliable estimates about drop-out rates at the end of the first and second years, these are generally based on past precedent. It can be argued that new factors such as the rapid expansion of student numbers over the past half decade, a rapidly reducing unit of resource, the growth of student poverty and labour market opportunities (or lack of them) may upset these calculations' (Bargh et al., 1994: 24–25).

As in further education, withdrawal rates and the timing of withdrawal can significantly affect an institution's core funding. There may also be a loss of tuition fee income from LEAs:

'The accuracy of the date recording when a student left a programme can affect the university as it determines whether the institution receives a tuition payment from the student's LEA' (Moore, 1995: 41).

Moore (1995) refers to an additional problem: unless students withdraw early enough for places to be filled again, there may be a loss of valuable places at a time when there has been an enforced contraction in higher education student numbers.

The recording of student retention and withdrawal rates has therefore taken on increasing importance in higher as well as further education. In both sectors, it is now as much in the institution's as in students' interests to minimise early withdrawal and funding criteria play a major role in this. Indeed, Hand, Gambles and Cooper (1994) argue that financial leverage has become a *force majeure* in post-compulsory education and training, obliging the three major 'stakeholders' – providers, funding 'clients' and learning 'customers' – to have an equally strong interest in course completion. They illustrate the point in relation to training programmes provided by government and employers:

'Clients, i.e. TECs and Unemployment and Benefit systems, can withhold payment to the provider and student against certain types of loss or withdrawal ... For the provider, this is a powerful incentive to minimise loss; for the customer, the threat

We need more clarity and consistency. Treating a student who has transferred onto another SHU programme as a withdrawal inflates the 'drop-out' rate needlessly. While it may be appropriate for different definitions to be used for different reports, we need to be clear in each case exactly what is being included in the figures' (Moore, 1995: 7, 43).

Reports to this project also suggest that different higher education faculties or departments interpret completion and withdrawal fairly generously. According to confidential information received from one university:

'Our unofficial policy (on post-degree level courses) is to consider all those who have paid their fees to have "completed" the course so long as they have attended some sessions. This is for funding reasons.'

Factors Which Complicate Measurement of Completion and Non-completion

The increasing flexibility conferred on individual learning patterns by credit transfer schemes, modularisation and different learning modes has made it difficult to fit student behaviour into narrow definitions of completion and non-completion. As a result of the way in which data are required, some practitioners, especially those working across institutions and sectors, complain that their non-completion rates appear unjustifiably high.

'We work with a variety of providers and organisations. No one has got a handle on completion. It is a complex situation, not controllable by any one model' (OCN representative).

Capizzi (1994) argues that traditional learning patterns involving groups of students following fixed, time-limited courses of study are gradually being eroded as the range of different learning options open to individuals increases. Yet quality indicators remain based on such traditional concepts:

'Within any credit accumulation scheme, students may be enrolling on a "course" or they may be collecting credits without an initial and clear intention of gaining the number and combination of credits that will/can constitute a particular programme of study. At some point that decision will be made but it is not necessarily the same point for all students.

Most (Access) courses permit some variation in what students undertake within the programme (whether simply through choice of modules or possibilities through APEL, APL, substitution, different combinations of credit levels and the levels at which work can be assessed). Hence students increasingly do not have the same "on programme" experience or achievements. Coherence is, therefore increasingly defined in relation to the students' learning experience rather than the programme delivery. Combine this with more flexible modes and lengths of attendance and one can see that the concept of a "cohort" of students is increasingly inappropriate at further and higher education levels. ... Pressures to modularise are powerful.

These developments have resulted in the "decomposition" of courses: they become collections of modules and credits. However, Access courses are required to have a "coherence" and have a "planned" programme of study and quality assessments at present still tend to focus upon the course/award rather than the individual. Traditional conceptions of a "cohort" of students following a "course" have been central to monitoring and remain part of the system of quality assurance' *(Capizzi, 1994: 292).*

Transfers

Transfers between learning modes, courses and institutions create particular problems for the measurement of completion and withdrawal rates, although they are allowed for in funding methodologies. FEFC Circular 93/31, for example, makes some provision for changes of learning mode and transfers within an institution:

'Where a student withdraws from only part of a programme, the mode of attendance and course group of the student should be reassessed in the light of the partial withdrawal. If this results in a change in the mode of attendance from full-time to part-time, then this should be recorded as a withdrawal and a transfer.

Enrolments at 1 November should be counted according to the mode of attendance and course group at 1 November. Transfers between programmes of study before 1 November should not be recorded as separate enrolments on returns.

For returns made later in the academic year such as the DFE return in the spring term 1993, a student who transferred between programmes of study would count as a withdrawal from the first programme and an additional enrolment on the second, only where that student changed from a full-time mode of attendance to a part-time or vice versa. A transfer involving a change in programme of study but not involving a change between full-time and part-time mode of attendance or vice versa, would not count as an additional enrolment or a withdrawal.'

traditionally been more relaxed in their approach, further and higher education are uncomfortable with a concept that does not easily accord with official definitions of non-completion:

> 'There is no distinction between "interrupted learning" and "dropping out". Those students who were not attending for the last third or so of the course would be considered to have dropped out although there are no guidelines on this' (HE representative).

A study at a further education college (Whittaker, 1994) concluded that, according to FEFC funding methodology, teaching time and attendance ratios would only be rewarded, in unit total calculations, in respect of 20 per cent of a small sample of former students. Those who had interrupted learning because of sickness or pregnancy, and those who had transferred to other institutions following residential moves, would be considered as 'drop-outs'. Furthermore, the intentions to return expressed by most of the students who had interrupted learning would not be valid as 'auditable evidence of an intention to return' since this only applies to a discrete course and not to a restart in the following academic year. Whittaker concluded from his study that current further education funding methodology takes no account of adult commitments and life patterns:

> 'Would colleges be better off not accepting students who are, or likely to be, pregnant, to get a job, become ill, go to another college, suffer domestic problems? There is an implicit conflict between the growth targets and the demands and realisation of ordinary people's lives, exacerbated by a narrow perception of outcomes which does not acknowledge the concept of interrupted learning so common among adult students. Essentially this flaw in the funding methodology works against part-time adult students, who are particularly likely to choose this mode to fit in with the other demands of their lives and whom we must cater for in increasing numbers to fulfil government targets' (Whittaker, 1994: 5).

This is unfair both to the institution and to the individuals concerned:

> 'No other outcomes are valid in terms of unit calculation and thus eventual funding. This raises serious questions when students have to change course or withdraw for reasons such as pregnancy or domestic problems. The notion of "drop-out" is particularly damaging to adults compared with other students. We need to demonstrate the concept of interrupted learning. We get unfairly penalised for people taking time off for living' (Whittaker, 1994: 5).

Some 'non-traditional' learners may take longer than the allocated time to complete courses and this can inflate an institution's non-completion rates:

> *'What if we include in "wastage" rate students who complete courses in longer than the stipulated time? This could lead to overestimate' (FE staff member).*

A follow-up study at a further education college also found that funding definitions do not always reflect mature student learning behaviour:

> *' "Drop-out" is defined usually as someone leaving before the end of the period paid for. Only one interviewee fell into this definition. The period paid for is open-ended up to a period of three years after the end of the course time in that students can complete any time within the three years. It therefore has to be questioned how far any of the "non-completing" students can be seen as drop-outs only a year after the end of their course' (Harvey, 1995a).*

Thus staff at institutions with high proportions of adult learners can find it difficult to match student learning patterns to the definitions and time-scales used in funding returns.

Positive Withdrawals

It is frequently pointed out that people sometimes leave programmes of study for *positive* reasons: because they have derived all the benefit they need or want; because they have realised that a course is not appropriate for them or because they have gained employment. In such cases, negative terms such as 'drop-out' do not strictly apply, as made clear in the following comments from the research literature and informants to this study:

> *'FEFC requirements don't take account of positive exits, such as for employment' (OCN representative).*

> *'If a student drops out of a course because he/she has acquired what they wanted, can they still be considered as drop-outs?' (Herrick, 1986: 22).*

> *' "Wastage" is not an appropriate term. Many (part-time degree students) who leave, subsequently return to some kind of academic or professional study; many leave for reasons peripheral to the course and its content; others leave because attendance achieves the career advancement they are seeking. Those who do leave because they can't cope with or don't enjoy*

the course may nevertheless gain from the experience' (Smith and Saunders, 1988: 32).

'The student who has got everything he or she requires from a course and therefore ceases to attend is surely both a completing and a successful student' (Mansell and Parkin, 1990: 23).

'Gaining a degree is not the only possible positive outcome from OU study. Some students gain a course credit or two then use them to transfer into a full-time degree course elsewhere. Others stop studying when they have learned as much as they want to. Rather than dismissing such students as "failures", we must consider why they stopped studying, what benefits they gained from study and what are their attitudes to further study' (Woodley, 1992: 117).

'Students were discontinuing, not drop-outs. Without exception respondents claimed that the course had left a positive legacy. Many expressed the desire to return when circumstances were more favourable' (Cullen, 1994: 12).

'Students can take away increased academic knowledge, some specified achievement or a better understanding of themselves, despite not formally completing' (Open University, West Midlands Region, 1995).

In its analysis of exit rates in the former polytechnic and college sector, the former Department of Education and Science also warned that withdrawal should not always be seen in a negative light:

'The exit rates reported here should not be interpreted as "wastage rates". Leaving a course is not synonymous with "dropping-out". Students who leave their original course may continue on a non-degree level course, may resit a year or may intend to return after taking time off' (DES, 1992).

Staying in the system

There is substantial evidence that many who leave a course or institution remain in the education system or have every intention of returning to learning at a future date. At the University of Lancaster, Taylor and Johnes (1991) found that 22 per cent of students who had withdrawn after starting in 1991 had completed a degree or diploma since leaving the university. Woodley (1992) found that very few 'dormant' Open University students surveyed had given up their undergraduate studies for good. A follow-up survey after a joint Open University/Coventry University study revealed that more than 90 per cent of former OU students had either resumed study or registered for other courses, while 90 per cent of former Coventry University part-time mature students were also studying elsewhere (*Times Higher*, 22 December 1995). According to a senior counsellor at the OU:

'What surprised me was that so many so-called "drop-outs" are actually back in. People aren't leaving education: they're shifting around.'

A survey of students who had withdrawn from courses at Liverpool John Moores University (LJMU) in 1992/93 indicated that 37 per cent of former full-time students had moved to another university and 12 per cent bad transferred to another course at LJMU; 37 per cent had found full-time employment and some had returned to study at a later date. Twenty-seven per cent of former part-time students had moved to another university and 49 per cent expressed an intention to return to education in the future (LJMU, 1995b).

Of former students tracked at Sheffield Hallam University, 70 per cent intended to return to higher education; 17 per cent thought they might return and only 8 per cent said they definitely would not (Moore, 1995).

It is abundantly clear, therefore, that people who leave a course of study have not always 'dropped out', although this is how it may appear from crude statistics. As a result, many teaching staff and those conducting institutional studies are increasingly avoiding the term 'drop-out' because of its negative connotations.

This prompts the conclusion that student withdrawal should not invariably be viewed as failure, either on the part of the individual or on the part of the institution, although league tables and the financial penalties imposed on institutions with high withdrawal rates encourage such a judgment. As argued by Davies and Yates (1987): 'the labels attached to outcomes of study such as "success", "failure", "completion" and "non-completion" are ambiguous and unsatisfactory', and now that completion rates have become a prime performance indicator in both further and higher education sectors, there are increasing calls for consistency and uniformity in the use of definitions and presentation of data:

'Until more progress is made towards agreement on common definition of terms and analysis of data each institution needs to make clear how any definitions were calculated. In papers, researchers must show their formulae for determining enrolment and withdrawal statistics and specify the points in time at which measurements were made.

In the long-run it is possible that there will be a trend towards greater commonality in definitions and recording procedures.

Governments are showing increasing interest in the use of performance indicators such as completion rates, in an effort to make educational institutions more accountable. Clearly performance indicators are of little value unless measured consistently. Part of the process of introducing them is, therefore, to decide on definitions, measuring procedures and reporting formats' (Kember, 1995: 29).

The next chapter will consider the procedures currently used by institutions for collecting student data and measuring and recording withdrawals.

Chapter 3

Data Collection: Scope, Methods and Purposes

The questionnaire sent to institutions sought to establish the kinds of data collection methods that were being employed by further and higher education institutions; the nature of the information on completion and non-completion collected and the purposes to which it was being put. The survey findings indicate that before 1994/95, little detailed information on student retention and withdrawal patterns was generally available, but that institutions are now beginning to collect more in response to the data requirements and targets of central funding bodies. However, some are experiencing difficulties in complying with data requirements and there are signs that tracking part-time students and those involved inflexible learning modes poses particular problems. In many institutions, computerised information systems do not have the capacity to record and retrieve the relevant data.

Until recently, the recording of student attendance and withdrawal patterns does not seem to have been a priority in any sector of post-compulsory education. Moreover, although there is some data on full-time students in conventional learning modes, little reliable information is available on different cohorts of students, especially adult learners in non-full-time and flexible provision.

Adult and Further Education

Data collection methods in local education authorities (LEAs) appear to be extremely variable and wide discrepancies have been found between central data and class registers. One informant analysed his Authority's information on completion in four different ways and got four different retention rates. Other informants admitted that there has been a tradition of organising adult programmes on the assumption that there will be a high withdrawal rate.

A recent NIACE project (NIACE, 1995) suggested that mechanisms for monitoring completion rates in further education colleges are also extremely variable, and that except for Access courses, arrangements for tracking the progression of adult learners are underdeveloped in many institutions. The comments of further education staff consulted for this project suggest that this reflects the general situation fairly accurately:

> *'Until recently no one has had any idea of retention or drop-out rates.'*

> *'The field isn't good at this. What's been done has tended to be one-off for funding purposes. Odds and ends of work have been done in corners of the system for local purposes but it's not coherent and hasn't been disseminated.'*

> *'To try and find out anything (on non-completion) in our college is very difficult.'*

The Further Education Funding Council has established a more rigorous data-collection system and it is expected that analysis of the individualised student record (ISR) returns will eventually yield a comprehensive national profile of student attendance patterns. Responses from colleges to this enquiry suggest that the new data requirements have been welcomed in some quarters:

> *'The FEFC is forcing us at last to consider this aspect (non-completion).'*

> *'The need to collect data has done us a lot of good. It could be important in ensuring that proper standards are applied.'*

Student data systems in further education

The computerised information systems in use in the colleges which responded to the survey included Femis, Microcompass College 2000 MIS system, CovTech Applications, DITA (Devon Information Technology Agency), Fretwell Downing, SIMS and other 'in-house bespoke' systems.

To meet FEFC data requirements, some of the responding colleges had recently changed their computerised information systems. Others were in the process of installing new systems or updating existing ones to increase their data-recording capacity:

> *'Our (Femis) system holds personal details, programme details and withdrawal details and is currently being expanded to include achievement results. A new system of monitoring student attendance was put in place in 1993/94.'*

Typically, the core information stored in the management information systems of the responding colleges includes the numbers of students by course and mode of attendance, leaving dates and reasons for withdrawal (including transfer).

The definitions of withdrawal used by responding colleges are, in virtually all cases, based on those used by the FEFC – non-attendance for four consecutive weeks – although one institution defined it as three weeks of unauthorised non-attendance. Another uses a cut-off period of 10 days' absence for TEC-funded students, while another employs a broader definition for non FEFC-funded students:

> *'A withdrawer is defined as any student who does not complete a course (i.e. stops attending prior to programme completion date if prior to gaining the intended qualification aim, whichever is appropriate).'*

Although most of the colleges contacted stated that they had incorporated monitoring and recording of completion rates into their strategic and operational planning procedures, few could supply statistical information on student completion and non-completion. Some respondents could provide limited data for the most recent academic year but this was invariably not in the detail required for this exercise:

> *'Our MIS is still evolving and data from three years ago is difficult or impossible to get hold of in spite of the massive proportion of adults in the college. This exercise (the NIACE survey) has thrown up some horrendous documentation.'*

Reasons for collecting data

All the colleges that responded to the survey stated that they were collecting and recording data on student attendance and non-completion to meet statutory funding and performance data requirements, and specifically FEFC requirements and targets.

> *'We collect data to ensure the accuracy of the three FEFC returns and to provide an auditable trail of evidence.'*

> *'Student withdrawal rates are used as part of institutional planning cycle, providing information for resourcing.'*

Several also referred to the data requirements of other funding bodies such as TECs and the Welsh Office.

The next most frequently mentioned reason for collecting data on completion rates was to maintain quality assurance or control. Most of the colleges referred to the use of such data in course management and review and in programme monitoring, evaluation and planning:

> *'The information is aggregated at appropriate levels of the college for monitoring and reporting purposes.'*

> *'Course/subject review sheets feed into the programme and course review procedure.'*

> *'Cohort analysis is an integral feature of course/curriculum monitoring, review and evaluation.'*

> *'Data is used to assist in the planning of future curricular programmes and to provide an informed statistical base from which to project learning unit targets. To assist the course review process by providing a detailed student profile of each course.'*

Data on retention and withdrawal do not seem to be widely used in staff appraisals, although in one college this forms part of staff appraisal for management spine staff, and in another, had been used in decisions on renewal of contracts: 'when part-time and fractional staff were invited to apply for fractional costs and upgrading on new conditions of service.'

Reflecting the findings of the NIACE further education project (1995), few colleges mentioned collecting data in order to assess student satisfaction and the extent to which they had been helped to realise their goals. However, four respondents stated that completion and non-completion data were used in the planning, evaluation and improvement of student support systems such as pastoral care and tutorial and academic skills provision. Another two were using the data to assist work on increasing retention rates.

Responsibility for collecting data

Responses to the question on who has responsibility for collecting the relevant data indicate that in most cases the information is collected by tutors and administrative staff in different departments and units, often in paper-based form such as withdrawal slips, and passed to Management Information Systems:

> *'Tutors; Students Records Unit.'*

> *'Academic schools via Registry.'*

> *'Lecturers pass to MIS via administration and Quality Assurance Team Monitor.'*

> *'Information is passed on to Head of school, course tutors and CMIS.'*

> *'Tutors and directors of study.'*

> *'All units pass information to FEMIS MIS officer.'*

> *'Personal tutors and/or community co-ordinators collect information then pass on to the Management Information Unit.'*

'Tutors pass to Registry to log onto SIMS.'

'Heads of school provide data to MIS, Campus offices and Registry.'

'Strategic responsibility (for collecting data) lies with the Associate Principal and operational responsibility with the Associate Director (CMIS) and team.'

'These Performance Indicators are collected at faculty, programme area, school, course and college site levels and fed into CMIS.'

'Data is collected at programme level and recorded in programme registers. The Quality Unit administers the system. The reasons for withdrawal are entered into the central system.'

'Our Enrolments and Register systems collect and record student data. This forms the core of MIS which automatically calculates completion and non-completion rates. We also use paper-based systems to support CMIS and as preparation for the three funding returns to FEFC.'

The evidence provided by colleges suggests that the accuracy of the information collected and recorded relies heavily on the vigilance and energy of individual tutors, the correctness of entries in registers, and the prompt notification of staff by students that they are intending to withdraw or have withdrawn from a programme – all of which leaves a large margin for potential error. As one sceptical informant commented:

'Student forms don't give an accurate picture or staff just put anything down.'

Advising and contacting non-completers

Institutions were asked what procedures were in place to contact students known to have withdrawn from a course or to advise those who had failed to attend for a significant period. The responses, some of which were cryptic, revealed variations in practice:

'Variable across college; under review.'

'Tutorial responsibility.'

'Tutors follow attendance guidelines.'

'Pastoral tutor contact for full-time and student services for part-time.'

'Students are contacted by letter, telephone and sometimes in person.'

requirements, and few could provide relevant and detailed information. A confidential report from an old university referred to cumulative problems relating to existing software, the new enrolment system, relocation of records and changes in procedures. Another university respondent admitted that his institution failed to collect 'full and accurate data on students' and that the collection and recording of data on student withdrawals 'had not been afforded the attention it should have received'. Research in individual institutions confirms that, until relatively recently, collecting data on withdrawal was not considered of primary importance in many higher education institutions:

> *'Recording the exact date and reason for withdrawal has not been a high priority in many parts of the university so figures are often inadequate. The current reality is that the data collected is flawed in many ways' (Moore, 1995: 41).*

Student data systems in higher education

As in further education, several institutions had changed, or were in the process of changing or adapting, their computerised information systems at the time of the enquiry:

> *'We use an in-house system, Sturec, for all full-time degree students but are transferring to a new system. The new computerised enrolments system is not yet fully operational.'*

Other systems mentioned were: 'Internal system: Streams'; CCSL Powerhouse Database; IBM and Microsoft Access version 2.0. One respondent referred to an integrated computerised admissions and student record system which enables personal details to be collected both at the applicant stage and annually at enrolment: 'Academic data is collected and confirmed annually at enrolment and also via academic departments throughout the year.'

All responding institutions were collecting data on student completion and withdrawals using HEFC (and HESA) definitions, cut-off dates and standard exit categorisations:

> *'We use HESA definitions: as long as students sit the first examination, they are considered to have completed that academic year.'*

> *'Student "counts" are conducted in compliance with Funding Council and HESA requirements. HEFC counts are undertaken in November and July and HESA returns produced in December.'*

> *'Non-completion includes voluntary and compulsory withdrawal and academic failure.'*

*'Non-completion rates calculated after end of session by gender,
fee status, and by three year averages.'*

Reasons for collecting data

The main reasons cited for collecting data on retention and non-completion were, firstly, to meet HEFC and HESA statistical requirements, and secondly, to contribute to planning, monitoring and quality assurance:

*'Maintaining accurate records is considered essential due to
funding imperatives; quality control/evaluation; development of
support structures; reduction of drop-out rate and instigation of
follow-up procedures; development of curricula, enlightenment
of pedagogical practices; research purposes.'*

*'To meet the requirements of outside agencies (HESA/HEFC)
and to support effective management and internal monitoring.'*

'Planning (intakes, projections), billing, performance analyses.'

*'Student tracking; financial administration; course administra-
tion; academic planning.'*

'Student records; to inform LEA/sponsors; internal monitoring.'

'Departmental reviews.'

One respondent claimed that such data was 'under constant review'.

Two of the responding institutions were not yet using data on retention and non-completion in their quality assurance procedures, although both intended to do so in the future:

*'We have plans to use this information as a factor in Performance
Indicators.'*

*'Student tracking data will eventually form part of departmental/
institutional quality reviews.'*

As with the further education responses, no respondents referred to the use of retention rates to check on the quality of student experience and satisfaction. One respondent admitted that this was considered to be a lower priority than funding and strategic planning:

*'In theory, this data is used in monitoring and development of
guidance, student support, equal opportunities and curriculum
development. In practice, funding and general planning are
probably more significant.'*

Responsibility for collecting data

In all the responding institutions, departments are expected to inform Academic Registries and student record offices of the date and reasons for withdrawal:

> *'The primary responsibility for official records rests with the Academic Registry. All suspensions/withdrawals/non-completions are recorded centrally as and when the Registry is notified by department/examining board.'*

However, the evidence both from the small sample of responding higher education institutions and from the research literature suggests that, at the time of the enquiry, student data were typically being collected in different ways by different people in different schools, departments and administrative areas, using different categorisations for different purposes. For example, one respondent from an old university admitted that data-gathering tends to be somewhat arbitrary and varies according to department, cohort of students and learning mode:

> *'Arrangements for recording student information are very varied and the situation very complex. The quality and accuracy of information is closely linked to the procedures advocated by the internal departments and by the commitment of individual tutors/lecturers to: (a) accurate recording of information, and (b) maintaining relatively close relations with their students. With Access students, for example, computerised records for the last two years have included details of completion, non-completion and withdrawals (although most of the reasons recorded are "never appeared" or "no reason given"). With part-time degrees, however, the situation is one of confusion. The data is currently recorded by the data unit when they have been informed by teaching staff but there are problems with timing and the accuracy of the reasons recorded. In our department, the secretary with responsibility for this area of provision keeps paper records in relation to withdrawn students. This creates an illusion of efficient record-keeping but is not very informative.'*

Similar admissions were made by several other respondents:

> *'Non-completion rates are not routinely calculated and full data has not been available in the past. Most data is recorded by secretaries at end of course/term/session.'*

> *'The information given is based on an informal enquiry involving members of staff directly involved with the mainly computerised recording of student data.'*

This corresponds with the picture described by Moore (1995: 90):

'Practice in tracking students differs between schools and pro-grammes within the schools. In some cases, there are no formal systems to record attendance. Some staff were able to report that they monitored attendance "rigorously", whilst others had no formal systems to record attendance. It was often felt that persistent absenteeism could fail to be noted, although much depended on the structure of the particular course of study. For instance, persistent non-attendance was more likely to be noted on a programme where group work was involved, such as on Science courses, than on other courses.'

Thus, as in further education, the accuracy of the data collected relies largely on individual departmental and staff practice and prompt student notification. However, some universities have found that many students disappear without informing staff and this creates great problems with the maintenance of accurate records:

'Some students negotiate either temporary leave of absence or permanent; others simply leave without informing anyone and departments follow them up as best they can when this is noticed.'

Advising and contacting non-completers

Strategies for advising and following up students who have left or who intend to withdraw also appear to vary widely both between and within higher education institutions. According to one respondent:

'Procedures vary from department to department and from tutor to tutor. In most courses, students advise tutors or confirm to staff that they have withdrawn. Some courses have student support structures which may result in earlier information.'

Other respondents referred (somewhat tersely in some cases) to procedures such as:

'Letters.'

'Letter from tutors and/or registry. No withdrawals encoded unless notified by students.'

'Interviews with senior tutor/welfare co-ordinator.'

'Guidelines in regulations.'

'Discussion with personal tutors, heads of department and relevant assistant principal.'

> *'A network of personal tutors/academic advisors/welfare officers/ professional counsellors is available at all times to advise students on their options.'*

In some of the responding institutions, there were no established procedures for contacting students:

> *'There is no procedure for chasing up non-attenders, although individual tutors might well choose to do this. Much of the information is dependent on the relationship between the tutor and the students and between the tutor and Departmental staff.'*

> *'In our department the nature of the course and individual priorities of tutors are key factors. In the university as a whole there seem to be no special procedures.'*

As these responses suggest, procedures to advise or contact actual or would-be leavers are largely dependent on staff knowing that a student has withdrawn or is intending to withdraw. In cases where students leave without informing the institution, there is a danger that their absence will not be noted until it is too late for follow-up procedures to be triggered, as two institutions have found:

> *'Although students are meant to inform the university when they leave, in practice, many disappear without informing anyone. If attendance is not monitored and absences acted upon, such a "disappearance" will not emerge until the Examination Board meets or when students fail to meet assessment deadlines.*
>
> *Twenty-one per cent (of non-completing students followed up) had left without discussing their situation with anyone from the institution'* (Moore, 1995: 26).

> *'Many students simply drop out or fail to return at the start of a new academic year without completing a withdrawal slip and therefore appear in these statistics as untraced'* (LJMU, 1995a: 3–4).

Some researchers have also found that contacting non-attenders is not a high staff priority:

> *'It is not standard practice in most schools to contact withdrawing students to check why they left or to ask them to confirm information received from academic staff. It was pointed out that administrative staff are often very busy and have not been encouraged to see this issue as important. One senior member of staff said that school staff are already fully occupied with looking after students who attend and so "problems" are not deemed to be worth wasting time over'* (Moore, 1995; 40–42).

Access Validating Agencies (AVAs)

Systems used for collecting and recording data

In 1993/94, the Continuing Education Research Unit at City University conducted surveys of AVAs (including Open College Networks) in order to establish the kind of information on Access courses and students they currently collect and record. This revealed extremely wide variations in data collection methods and information systems and, consequently, 'tremendous scope for inaccuracy in the recording of data'. The survey showed that the different agencies are funded and managed so differently, and their computer support services are so diverse, that it is very difficult to obtain comparable data:

> 'AVAs have radically different funding and resources, staff and equipment. As in all sectors of education, computerisation has tended to be ad hoc and a case of serendipity regarding whether, when and what hardware and software have been adopted. In 1993, 67.7 per cent reported relying on purely manual systems. By 1994, a bare majority reported continued reliance on manual systems, with significant numbers noting planned computerisation in the next year. This may, however, be a misrepresentation since some respondents would regard records kept on a word-processing system as a "manual" system; while others register that as computerisation. Nevertheless it is clear that only a small minority have access to or make use of database or spreadsheet systems that allow for any degree of systematic compilation and analysis of statistical data' (Capizzi, 1994: 291–292).

The study revealed that despite the requirement to produce detailed annual reports for HEQC, there was some confusion within AVAs about the kind of data required and whose responsibility it was to collect it. This was resulting in some duplication of data-gathering activities within providing institutions:

> 'By requiring annual reports that include data on enrolments, completions and achievement of certificates analysed in terms of gender, age, ethnicity, etc., AVAs have in many cases instituted the annual collection of such data. The HEQC system for review of AVAs also generates an opportunity for AVAs to assess what information is pertinent.
>
> It was not clear what data was already required and collected, and by whom at the institutional level. Ethnic monitoring, FESR returns and other requirements may be met by Access tutors' returns or may be undertaken by other staff in the institutions

themselves. In many institutions there is significant duplication of effort in collecting and analysing student records. The implementation of MIS won't ensure that this doesn't occur. Nor does the consolidation of FEFC and HESA requirements guarantee that appropriate data for monitoring quality will be collected' (Capizzi, 1994: 289).

Problems with Collecting Data

Thus, a common theme in responses to this enquiry was the difficulties post-compulsory providers are experiencing in collecting student data. According to a higher education respondent, the collection of such data has been hindered by a whole range of problems such as staff workloads, staff resistance to monitoring and quality control procedures, the difficulties of obtaining information from part-time tutors, resistance from students and their tendency not to divulge the real reasons for withdrawal.

In some cases, the main problem was inadequate information systems or changes to new systems that were not yet fully operational:

> *'It is difficult to produce an even comparison between the number of early leavers for 1992/93 and 1993/94 as a new system of monitoring student attendance is in place' (FE respondent).*

> *'MIS data seem unlikely to understand drop-out rates. There is over-estimation of student numbers and discrepancies between MIS data and registers because some students enrol for classes which they neither attend nor claim a refund for, and some last minute switches of classes' (Beddow, 1994).*

A number of informants in both sectors argued that the information systems currently in use were developed to deal with traditional students in conventional full-time courses. They were not designed to work with flexible study modes, interrupted learning and delayed completion, therefore cannot cope with students who transfer between programmes, shift from full- to part-time learning or take a temporary break from study. In consequence, several respondents to this project admitted that their conventional data-gathering systems cannot yet pick up enough detail to give a clear and accurate picture of student attendance patterns:

> *'It would be a major job to change the statistical structure of our data collection systems.'*

> *'Our system can't cope: all non-completers come out as withdrawers.'*

According to one respondent, about a third of all FEFC-funded organisations are having difficulty providing the requisite information for Individualised Student Records:

'One of the difficulties with FE data collection is that standard packages weren't designed for this purpose. They were designed for standard full-time students. Now that FEFC is driving the system away from a course focus to focus on individual students, colleges are trying to do three things: to adapt the unadaptable, investing in new software as an add-on, or going back to Square One: scrapping the lot and starting again from scratch.'

The scale of the problem has been demonstrated by audit findings indicating that many colleges are failing to count their student numbers accurately. According to the first full external audit of colleges' funding claims, 169 had their audit reports 'qualified' for such reasons as duplication of student enrolments, double counting of franchise students, inaccurate recording of withdrawals, errors in modes of attendance and use of estimates rather than actual student numbers. Additional problems were reported with software and failure to retain adequate supporting documentation (Utley, 1995b).

Problems have also been experienced in higher education, where:

'many of the existing methods of collecting and handling data on student progress were developed to deal with students following fixed courses of study. Now that is becoming increasingly flexible, these methods are often inappropriate: students who exercise choice, e.g. by transferring between programmes, by shifting between full-time and part-time study, or by withdrawing temporarily, can cause problems for these systems, which were not designed to work with such changes' (Moore, 1995: 40–41).

It has been reported that higher education institutions' inability to keep track of students has created problems for the Student Loan Company, which has found institutions reluctant to establish mechanisms for monitoring attendance because of the practical difficulties involved (*Times Higher*, 24 November 1995).

Particular difficulties in recording data were reported by organisations such as open college networks and access consortia which deal with different sectors and institutions. These are exacerbated in the case of part-time students and modular programmes:

'MIS need to encompass mobility and choice. The notion of a student accumulating credit and moving across the system is beyond their scope' (OCN representative).

'Institutions record part-time enrolments differently and there's been some unjustifiable increase of non-completion rates because

of the way the FEFC demands data. There are differences in the way people keep records: for example institutions record part-time enrolments differently. A lot of AVAs which have OCNs find it difficult to provide information on a course basis because of modular systems' (Capizzi, 1994: 292).

A respondent from an open college network also referred to the difficulties of tracking students caused by 'extreme patterns of discontinuous attendance among adults, particularly women.'

This study was undertaken at a time when institutional record-keeping was in a transitional stage and colleges and universities were moving towards fulfilling the more detailed data requirements of the new central bodies FEFC and HESA, although many seemed to be experiencing major problems in storing the relevant data on their current information systems. It is now up to FEFC and HEFC statisticians to encourage institutions to provide clearer and more detailed evidence on non-completion rates. There are hopes that FEFC requirements will lead to greater coherence and uniformity in the data provided by further and adult education institutions. When the ISR returns are analysed, there will be more detailed information providing evidence of the scale of non-completion in further education.

Similarly, it is hoped that the new, single and multi-purpose data-collection system covering the higher education sector – HESA – should be able to provide more detailed student data and a more thorough and coherent approach to collecting data in institutions.

In a year or two, therefore, more detailed data on retention and non-completion rates should be available. This ideally would include the exact number and dates of withdrawals as well as distinguishing between the different withdrawal paths taken by students (e.g. permanent withdrawal; delayed completion; transfers between courses and learning modes). It would also be useful to have this information disaggregated by programme and student characteristics such as age, gender, etc. However, there are worries that central data requirements do not include all the data considered important by providers and tutors. It was clear from institutional responses that although stress on student experience and support may be an important by-product of the need to monitor retention rates, the current moves towards data collection are fundamentally audit- and funding-driven. Thus, as Capizzi (1994) warns in relation to Access students, the creation of 'monolithic' data sets may not provide a totally comprehensive picture of student characteristics and experience. She argues that the data requirements of HESA and FEFC, albeit fairly detailed, are not always appropriate for mature students and concentration on them might elbow out the monitoring of other important areas such as equal opportunities and students' background and characteristics:

'It seems probable that FEFC and HEFC data requirements will govern the data collected by institutions. The resources required to develop and administer this information will take priority. Thus it seems likely that the only information kept will be that required by these systems. The monitoring of fields important for Access providers may become more rather than less problematic, for example the effectiveness of equal opportunities policies and targeting in FE.

The type of information on social background of students to be collected is particularly inappropriate for mature students. There will be no data collected on employment status, nationality, occupation, marital status, existence of dependants, etc. Disability is recorded only as "disabled registered or not registered" (although this is being consulted on). The FEFC system does, however, provide some opportunities for monitoring of students' educational background. Institutions will be required to enter the date when specific "entry qualifications" were gained. This will be particularly relevant as "a long break from study" is an important characteristic of Access students and this data could have value when monitoring targeting. Although most AVAs collect information on gender, age, ethnicity and disability, very few collect data on educational background and occupation.

HESA will operate as a more multi-function database and therefore seeks greater detail on student background including occupational status, nationality and more refined categories of disability. Nevertheless, it too seems to premise the typical student as an 18–21-year-old' (Capizzi, 1994: 293–294).

This is worrying, since the presence, in further and higher education, of a more diverse student body suggests the need for a cohort approach to the collection of student data. If non-completion rates are as high as generally believed, greater efforts will be required to identify and record the characteristics, experience and progress of specific cohorts of students.

Firstly, however, there is a need to determine what the non-completion rates actually are.

Chapter 4

Non-completion Rates

Although non-completion rates in both further and higher education are believed to be high, opinions differ on the actual percentage of withdrawals. The figures available nationally are inadequate, and comparisons between institutional figures are problematic because of differences between data collection methods and variations in the way institutions define and measure non-completion. Comparisons between research findings are also difficult because of their diversity and variations in the definitions of withdrawal used. As a result, the non-completion rates revealed by institutions and research investigations are too diverse to be conclusive.

There is a widespread perception that the 'wastage' rate from further and higher education is unacceptably high.

Concern about completion rates in further education has been expressed by both the Audit Commission (1993) and the Chief Inspector in the first annual FEFC report (1993). A report on statistical trends in post-16 education and training has been quoted as revealing:

> *'worsening drop-out rates in further education and a low 17-plus participation rate (which) points to low successful completion rates in all types of courses and problems of progression, particularly from NVQ Level 2 to Level 3' (Utley, 1995a).*

There has also been considerable media comment on allegedly high withdrawal rates from higher education, much of it linked to the rapid expansion of the sector, which has not met with universal approval. One highly critical article has claimed that: 'a disturbingly high proportion of students are dropping out' (Clare, 1995).

Definitive figures on 'wastage rates' are, however, extremely hard to find and estimates vary widely. As recently as 1993, the Audit Commission described as 'disturbing' the lack of basic data that would enable an analysis of the numbers of successful, unsuccessful and non-completing 16–19-year-old students on courses (Audit Commission, 1993).

Similarly, researchers invariably complain that national sets of data are scanty and often contradictory. For example, in their study

of alternative entry routes into higher education, Webb *et al.*
(1994) typically found 'major problems of comparability and compatibility'
between the data collected for the Universities Statistical Record, the
Further Education Statistical Record, the Polytechnics and Colleges
Funding Council and the Initial Teacher Training Clearing House:

> *'Analysis of national statistics highlighted the incompatibility
> of the various sets of data, which made it impossible to obtain
> a comprehensive and reliable picture of alternative entry to
> higher education across the United Kingdom or even England
> and Wales ... Clear, reliable data is just not available' (ibid.,
> 1994: 4, 13).*

A number of people consulted for this project also expressed
strong views on the dearth of national data:

> *'Our national data system is appalling.'*

> *'We desperately need a national data base. We should be lob-
> bying for national student numbers.'*

> *'What can be said sensibly on a national basis about mature
> student retention is nil!'*

Although individual institutions can produce average non-
completion figures for particular years, there are difficulties in comparing the raw data because of the differences between institutions and
variations in their data collection methods and in their definitions of,
and ways of measuring, non-completion. Some institutional figures
include all types of withdrawal including academic failure and transfers; others exclude transfers and other forms of non-completion. This
leads to wide diversity in the quality and quantity of data available.

Smith and Saunders (1991) also found substantial variations
between institutions in the methods and time-scales employed in
calculating non-completion rates after the first year of study. Other
researchers have found that even comparing first-year rates can be
problematic since, as Webb *et al.* (1994) point out, student data is a
'point of time issue' which is:

> *'constantly being updated as missing information becomes
> available and as students' circumstances change, particularly,
> in the first year as they change course and or subject.'*

These researchers concluded that without central guidance on
the collection and recording of information, the accuracy of existing data would be open to question:

> *'The lack of central guidance with regard to the compilation of
> the FESR and the consequent variation in practice at institutional
> level raise questions about the validity of aggregated national*

FESR data and the comparability of institutional data' (Webb
et al., 1994: 11).

The research literature on student progress fills some but not all
of the gaps. This is composed largely of institutional studies involving one or a small number of institutions. These vary widely in the
research methods used and in the size of research samples. There
are also some broader national studies of adult learners such as
Woodley *et al.* (1987) and studies of specific cohorts such as
Access, 'alternative entry' and part-time degree students. However,
it has been observed that:

> '*Research on the experiences of mature students tends to be
> qualitative and is rarely set within a framework of national and
> institutional data collection and policy-making' (Webb et al.,
> 1994: 28).*

Definitions of Adult Students

For those seeking data on adult students, an added difficulty is
created by the fact that the term 'adult' is variously defined. In further education, mature students are generally considered to be those
aged over 19, while in higher education they are generally defined
as people aged over 21 on undergraduate and sub-degree courses:

> '*The university defines mature students as those aged 21 or
> more at entry. It does not break down maturity into higher age
> cohorts' (Moore, 1995).*

The definition of a mature student as someone aged over 21 may
not lead to useful comparisons since students in their early twenties
are likely to have more in common with standard-aged students than
with those in their thirties, forties or fifties. Thus Webb *et al.* (1994)
describe official categories of mature students as 'too inclusive to be
analytically useful' and it has been suggested that, in order to make
meaningful comparisons between students, it would be necessary to
focus on specific sub-groups such as Access students, mature women
students and people entering programmes through non-standard
routes (Metcalf, 1993). While there have been a few research studies
of some of these groups, few institutions collect cohort-based data of
this kind.

Adult Non-completion

There are few recent figures available specifically on adult non-
completion rates. In the 1994 MOM poll (NIACE, 1994), about
15 per cent of the people surveyed said they had withdrawn

from some courses before completion. However, figures based on self-reported behaviour cannot be relied upon to be accurate and the student sample included people under 20.

There are no reliable national statistics on withdrawal rates from adult education classes and the few national studies with this kind of information are now somewhat dated. These suggest that rates of early withdrawal from adult provision have tended to be relatively high but with very wide variations between geographical areas and types of course. The NIAE national survey (1970), for example, found that non-completion rates for vocational courses ranged from 30 per cent to 80 per cent and for non-vocational from 11 per cent to 26 per cent. A later study (which involved a sample of 3,000 students in over 150 evening courses lasting two terms) suggested that the average early leaving rate was 21 per cent in the first term ('drop-out' being defined as a failure to attend any of the last four meetings of the Autumn term). However, the researchers then found that a massive 58 per cent of those who had initially enrolled in the Autumn term had not re-enrolled (Woodley *et al.*, 1987).

Studies in individual areas have inevitably revealed widely differing completion rates. Research into withdrawal from non-vocational classes provided by the Northamptonshire adult education service in 1985/86 revealed a withdrawal rate of just under 20 per cent (Herrick, 1986). A lower rate of 15.5 per cent was found in another study in the Huddersfield area. This covered 8,000 evening class students in 395 courses over a four-year period. and 'drop-out' was defined as a student who left a course three weeks or more before the end of the period paid for (Roberts and Webb, 1979).

A pilot evaluation of the adult evening curriculum (149 courses) conducted at a tertiary college between 1993 and 1994, revealed an even lower rate of withdrawal – 8 per cent – the largest number in GCSE/GCE classes (Beddow, 1994).

High withdrawal rates have been recorded for students involved in adult basic education classes. One study (Sanders, 1977) refers to a 39 per cent withdrawal rate from one-to-one classes in the Manchester area.

The diversity of these findings demonstrates that variables such as geographical location, type of institution and course inevitably affect attendance patterns. This in turn demonstrates the difficulty of reaching meaningful general conclusions about adult completion rates.

Further Education

As in adult education, there are few reliable statistics available on completion and non-completion in further education. In June 1995, the only national figure available from the FEFC Statistics Branch was 10 per cent but this related only to full-time, whole-year students in 1993/94. No national figures are available relating specifically to the completion rates of mature students. There have, however, been some general studies of non-completion in further education, some specifically on students aged 16–19 and those on courses leading to specific qualifications.

According to one report (Mansell and Parkin, 1990), withdrawal rates of 30 per cent are generally regarded as standard for further education students who are not sponsored by their employers. However, this relates only to first-term withdrawals: in subsequent terms, the authors claim, the rate rises steeply:

'The 30 per cent "norm" which is quite widely acknowledged in the system, seems in practice to relate to first-term drop-out, perhaps under the influence of the traditional spot-check date at the beginning of November. In practice, drop-out rates by the second term can reach into the 40 or 50 per cent ranges, with even higher rates of drop-out recorded in term 3. For the courses we have surveyed, the highest final drop-out rate, of 80 per cent, was reached for a part-time evening course' (Mansell and Parkin, 1990: 5).

An HMI (1991b) report on completion rates in further education suggested a lower average rate than the Mansell and Parkin findings although high rates were recorded for particular courses. This survey found that 13 per cent of a sample of students from a range of different courses had withdrawn by the end of six months, but that the leaving rate reached 40 per cent on some courses. The report refers to previous HMI findings that up to 25 per cent of students were failing to complete A-level programmes. The Audit Commission (1993) study of 16–19-year-old students also revealed wide variations according to the type of course: non-completion rates averaged about 13 per cent for A-level courses and 18 per cent for vocational courses. However, on individual courses in particular institutions the early leaving rate could be as high as 80 per cent, giving cause for alarm:

'Similar proportions of enrolled students complete courses but fail to achieve their main intended aims. Losses on this scale justify increased efforts to persuade more students to complete their courses and to match students and courses more appropriately.

On a national level, extrapolation from the fieldwork sample suggests that of the order of 150,000 young people each year are leaving full-time courses without achieving what the course was designed for, either through leaving early or through failure in the relevant examinations and assessments' (Audit Commission, 1993: 2, 24).

High withdrawal rates have also been reported by BTEC (Smith and Bailey, 1993), whose study, using data based on 2,170 students from 254 programmes, showed that 44 per cent of both certificate and diploma students had left early, mainly for programme-related reasons. More recently, the Further Education Unit (1994) reported that the average 'drop-out' rate from GNVQ Level 2 is about 20 per cent and about 16 per cent for the first year of GNVQ Level 3. In the summer of 1995, it was alleged that up to two-thirds of all those taking GNVQs 'drop out' – a phenomenon attributed by the then Minister of State Lord Henley to the newness of the qualification and the fact that some students take it part-time while others transfer to A-levels (BBC Radio 4, *Today Programme*, 21 August 1994).

These findings display the usual wide variations, and some analysts have reported a much lower withdrawal rate from examination courses than others (for example Payne, 1995). As suggested earlier, such variations often arise from differences in data collection methods and presentation – a situation that hinders any attempt to arrive at definitive conclusions about withdrawal rates.

Few figures were supplied by individual colleges that responded to this project. Two-thirds of respondents said that detailed information was not currently available or not held in a form to meet the request. Two reported that the only data collected were for full-time students and another that the only statistics available on mature students were for Access students. One respondent claimed that only the most recent information had any level of reliability or detail, while another commented that 'to get figures about people actually on course is absolutely hopeless'. Another reported that withdrawal rates at his college had fallen by over 20 per cent in the last few years but offered no explanation for this change.

Higher Education

In higher education the national data available on non-completion is limited and often restricted to students on full-time, first degree courses. The institutional statistics used frequently fail to distinguish between permanent and temporary withdrawals, withdrawal because of academic failure and voluntary withdrawal.

National data

A Department of Education and Science analysis of withdrawals of first-year students on full-time degree or sandwich courses in the polytechnic and college sector in 1987/88 revealed an overall 'exit rate' of 16 per cent. Seventy-eight per cent of these were identified as students terminating their studies because of academic failure or for the other categories of reasons listed in the Continuous Student Record. A further 10 per cent had transferred to another course (within the same institution), and 11 per cent intended to return to their studies after a temporary absence (DES, 1992).

Department for Education figures for the whole sector during the period 1983/84 to 1993 indicate that the overall rate of withdrawal fluctuated but generally remained under 20 per cent. Between 1983 and 1992/93, the number of students on full-time and sandwich first degree courses leaving because of examination failure, ill health, personal and other reasons, and those switching to a lower level courses, varied between 14 per cent and 17 per cent (Table 3). These figures exclude students transferring between degree courses or subjects and there is no disaggregation by age, sex or entry qualification (DFE, 1993).

Taylor and Johnes (1989) estimated that the average undergraduate non-completion rate in UK universities was about 18 per cent (although other academics have disagreed with this figure and the methods and analysis used).

In recent years there have been a series of contradictory reports and articles about student withdrawal from higher education, some of which maintain that 'drop-out' rates are unacceptably high. The *Push*

Table 3. *Full-time and sandwich first degree drop-out rates, percentages[1].*

Academic Year	83/84	84/85	85/86	86/87	87/88	88/89	89/90	90/91	91/92	92/93
Higher education	14	15	14	16	17	14	16	15	17	17

1. Drop-out covers all those leaving degree courses because of exam failure, ill health, personal and other reasons. It includes those switching to a lower level course but it excludes students transferring between degree courses or subjects.

The rate for each academic year reflects the progression of students through the whole length of the courses. The rate is a weighted sum of the separate university and former polytechnic figures based upon graduate numbers. It therefore excludes first degree students in other UK HE institutions. The calculation for the polytechnic drop-out rate is necessarily approximate because of significant limitations in the underlying date. In practice it has been necessary to estimate the drop-out in 1991/92 and 1992/93 from the change in two successive years for a sample of around half of the 29 English former polytechnics.

Sources: Universities' Statistical Record leavers and enrolment records; CNAA enrolment records England and Wales (1983/84 to 1990/91); DFE Further Education Statistical Record England (1991/92 to 1992/93).

Guide to Which University 95 (1994) reported a 15 per cent increase in non-completion rates, According to the Guide, more than one in eight students and more than one in five in some institutions had failed examinations or withdrawn from courses in 1992. This contrasts with the claim by the *Times 1994 Good Universities Guide* that undergraduate completion rates had 'increased dramatically' compared with those reported in their previous edition: '61 universities achieved completion rates of 90 per cent or better, compared with 33 in the previous year'. According to Moore (1995), the discrepancy between these conclusions could have more to do with changes in the methods of calculating figures than with any dramatic improvement in university performance.

The *Push Guide* was based on figures drawn from University Management Statistics and Performance Indicators (UMSPI) which, until recently, referred only to the old universities. The Committee of Vice-Chancellors and Principals (CVCP), which uses the same figures, disputed that there had been a sharp increase, claiming that the rate was constant at around 13 per cent and compared very favourably with those in other countries:

> '*Our figures show that the volume of students successfully graduating is 87 per cent which has remained constant for years. A 13.2 per cent drop-out rate is nothing to be ashamed of' (quoted in* Times Educational Supplement, *19 August 1994).*

The Department for Education (1995) also claimed that the figures appear low by international standards. Similarly, Benn (1994) has argued that compared with other countries in Europe, the rates of withdrawal from courses at UK universities have been relatively low. She attributes this to the fact that the British higher education system has traditionally been characterised by highly selective admission procedures, low participation, small class size, low student–teacher ratio and a tutorial system. However, recent changes such as expansion in numbers and the widening composition of the student body are inevitably leading to higher non-completion rates.

The CVCP has admitted that there has been an increase in the number of students withdrawing from courses, although they are at pains to relate the figures to the 13 per cent average for a three-year period:

> '*About 40,000 students at UK universities left their courses in 1992/93, a rise of nearly 25 per cent over the previous year – representing about 5 per cent of the total student population, although some may return in future years.*
>
> *The 13 per cent figure refers to a three-year student cohort. The present figure refers to a one-year period and is roughly*

Variations Between Subjects

One point on which the evidence is broadly consistent is that there are wide disparities in completion rates and overall performance between subjects. Most information on this issue comes from higher education, where a number of reports indicate that the retention of students, and particularly mature students, is poorer in science, engineering and technology subjects than in arts, social sciences and vocational subjects. Statistics also suggest a high rate of 'wastage' from law degrees.

The DES study of all first degree and sandwich students in polytechnics and colleges (DES, 1992) found wide variations in completion rates between subjects, with technology and science having about twice the 'exit' rate of music and drama courses. Withdrawals from first degree initial teacher training courses (which had a higher number of students aged over 22) were 4 per cent lower than exit rates for all types of first degree students (Table 4).

From their analysis of national figures for the 1970s, Woodley *et al.* (1987) concluded that mature students were most likely to gain a degree if they were studying a social science subject and least likely if they were taking science. Those taking arts subjects were almost twice as likely to gain a good degree as those taking science.

Similarly, a study of first year results among mature students taking accelerated (two-year) degree courses showed that the

Table 4. *First year first degree students, exit rates by subject and gender, percentages.*

	Men	Women	Both
Education	17	10	12
Medicine	14	11	12
Technology	25	21	24
Agriculture	6	–	4
Science	21	15	19
Business studies	18	13	15
Professional studies	19	13	16
Languages	17	15	16
Arts	15	12	13
Music, drama	9	9	9
All subjects	**19**	**12**	**16**

Source: DES Statistical Bulletin 9/92.

non-completion rate was much higher in science, engineering and technology than in other subjects (Foong *et al.*, 1994).

Institutional studies reveal a similar subject split as demonstrated by the following examples.

A study of the performance of mature students at the University of Warwick (Walker, 1975) indicated that mature students performed best in arts courses and least well when studying science courses.

At the Open University, Woodley and Parlett (1983) found that the 'wastage' rates for mathematics and technology courses were consistently above average at each of the course levels, and that those for arts and social science were consistently below average.

A study of former Access students in higher education (Davies and Yates, 1987) revealed a high rate of progression in vocational subjects, social studies, education, language and arts but a much lower one in science, technology and engineering.

Research at Sheffield Hallam University (Moore, 1995), showed that the largest number of withdrawn students had been in the School of Science.

An analysis of retention and success rates for the 1990 cohort of full-time degree students at Liverpool John Moores University revealed that the School of Art, Media and Design then had the highest retention rate and the School of Engineering and Technology Management the lowest. There were, however, wide differences between other subjects in the number of recorded student withdrawals in the first and later years of study (LJMU, 1995a).

Some of the survey responses to this enquiry revealed a broadly similar picture. One old university, for example, supplied information on the 1992/93 session which showed a first-year withdrawal rate of about 9 per cent from arts programmes but about 22 per cent from science programmes.

Press reports have expressed concern at high withdrawal rates from particular subject areas. One (Clare, 1995) quotes an inspectors' report which referred to 'unacceptably high wastage rates' in university engineering and architecture departments.

The evidence on differential retention rates between subjects in further education is both more sparse and less consistent. HMI (1991b) found that the subjects with the worst record of non-completion were art and design and business studies and the best, construction. A college which responded to this enquiry also claimed there were retention problems in business studies and humanities. Several others referred to 'subject variations' which were not made explicit.

At Wirral Metropolitan College in 1993/94, the highest percentage of early leavers were in the areas of continuing and general education, art, design and creative studies and personal and community studies (Wirral Metropolitan College, 1994).

In adult education, language courses are frequently cited as having a high withdrawal rate (Woodley *et al.*, 1987; Hamblin, 1990).

Whole sector statistics relating to particular subject areas need to be treated with caution since overall withdrawal figures can be distorted by particularly high rates at individual institutions:

> *'The non-completion rate for law is more than twice the average for other subjects. However, differences between the mean average rate and the worst case within each subject area are far greater than any differences between the means of different subject areas' (Smith and Saunders, 1991: 34).*

Similarly, a high rate of withdrawal from one or two subject areas can grossly distort an institution's overall withdrawal rate. For example, disaggregated data supplied for this project by an institute of higher education showed a high overall rate of withdrawal among part-time students in one particular year. All of these were from a single subject area. Other institutions have noted similar findings:

> *'The overall (withdrawal) percentage conceals a range of dropout rates across courses, with many, particularly vocational courses, having very successful outcomes' (Beddow, 1994).*

As Herrick (1986) argues, average student withdrawal rates are meaningless as they obscure the fact that there are courses where no one drops out and others where many students leave.

Type of Course and Learning Mode

Research studies indicate that other variables such as the type, level and length of courses, the learning mode employed and the current stage of a student's programme of study can also affect non-completion rates:

> *'Graduate programs tend to have lower attrition rates than first degrees. Longer programs usually have lower completion rates than short ones ... Within a course, attrition is usually higher, and often much higher, in the early stages than towards the end' (Kember, 1995: 24).*

Studies of completion of adult education courses have consistently found the highest rate of withdrawal to be from academic (qualifying) courses, rather than from general uncertificated programmes (Hamblin, 1990; Beddow, 1994).

Accelerated degree courses (which attract mainly mature students) have higher withdrawal rates (15 per cent) than parent (standard length) courses (9 per cent) (Foong *et al.*, 1994).

Distance learning has a higher withdrawal rate than other forms of provision. This is unsurprising, given that distance learning students are often working largely on their own and fitting study in with their other commitments. A joint study of non-completion among mature part-time undergraduates conducted by the Open University (West Midlands Region) and Coventry University revealed considerable differences in withdrawal rates, particularly in the social sciences where the Open University lost considerably more students than Coventry – 17 per cent as opposed to 6 per cent. However, the analysis showed that the two institutions were attracting very different student constituencies: one with strong vocational motives (Coventry) and one with more general educational motives (the Open University). Moreover, over the two-year period Coventry University recruited almost twice the number of students as the Open University (Open University, West Midlands Region, 1995).

Contrary to general assumptions, greater flexibility, though it greatly assists access, does not necessarily lead to better retention rates. Some higher education staff have found modular and combined degree courses lead to student isolation and have a high withdrawal rate. A study in Scotland found that students taking modular programmes had difficulty in consolidating knowledge and bringing together disparate elements and that they felt disadvantaged in relation to other students (Munn, MacDonald and Lowden, 1992).

Part-time study

The majority of part-time students in higher education are mature (Tight, 1991). It has been claimed that little is known about non-completion rates among this group (Bourner *et al.*, 1991), which Smith and Saunders (1991) attribute to the fact that the figures are 'notoriously difficult to calculate':

> *'Unlike full-time degree programmes where the majority of students complete the course in successive years, many part-time students spread their education over a longer period, sometimes moving between institutions' (Smith and Saunders, 1991: 31–33).*

There is nevertheless some evidence (Tight, 1991 refers to it as 'a commonplace') that part-time students have a higher withdrawal rate than those learning full-time. Smith and Saunders (1991), for example, allege that 'wastage rates for part-time degrees are undoubtedly higher on average than for full-time courses'. Their study of 235 part-time degree courses in 1986 found an average 'wastage' rate of 24 per cent during the first year, with one 'extreme report of 91 per cent':

> *'Part-time programmes tend to have numbers of students who drop out in the first one or two weeks and never register. On almost all part-degrees, most drop-out occurs in the first year'* (*Smith and Saunders, 1991: 31–33*).

Figures supplied for this study from an institute of higher education with a largely mature student body show a very low rate of withdrawal from full-time programmes but a sharply higher rate for part-time students:

1992–93

Male withdrawals:

- Full-time: 4.1 per cent of total roll
- Part-time: 21.1 per cent of total roll

Female withdrawals:

- Full-time: 5.3 per cent of total roll
- Part-time: 11.4 per cent of total roll

1993–94

Male withdrawals:

- Full-time: 5 per cent of total roll
- Part-time: 16 per cent of total roll

Female withdrawals:

- Full-time: 4.8 per cent of total roll
- Part-time: 10.6 per cent of total roll

Other higher education studies, however, have revealed withdrawal rates which are not significantly higher than those for full-time students. A longitudinal study of 1,600 part-time, mainly mature male students taking a Diploma in Management Studies (Bord, 1988) found that by the beginning of the second year, 18 per cent had left, 12 per cent of them in the first term of the first year.

Davies and Yates (1987) reported that 18.3 per cent of a small sample of former Access students who were taking higher education courses on a part-time evening basis withdrew without being assessed in at least one unit, usually within the first two semesters. A further 6.7 per cent successfully completed some units but subsequently chose to discontinue.

A survey of about 3,000 part-time mature undergraduates on 66 part-time CNAA degree programmes (Bourner *et al.*, 1991) revealed that, one year after enrolment, 11 per cent had withdrawn without any form of award; 3 per cent had failed; and 1 per cent had left with an intermediate award. This was perceived as very low compared with the figures produced by other studies.

Smith and Saunders (1991) noted that withdrawal rates from part-time programmes vary according to the time of day when courses are held:

> *'National data based on less than half of universities and three-quarters of polytechnics suggest that the mean first-year non-completion rate for all daytime courses is 16.9 per cent compared with 23.2 per cent for day and evening and 25.4 per cent for evening only, therefore the chances of survival are higher for day-time attendance. It also suggests that survival chances on evening classes are higher in the university sector' (Smith and Saunders, 1991: 32).*

The vulnerability of part-time evening courses to high withdrawal has been noted in other studies (Vinegrad, 1980; Davies and Yates, 1987), although it is not clear to what extent it is the time of day that affects withdrawal rates rather than other factors such as difficulties with the subject matter, workload, teaching styles, etc. It can also be assumed that many people who can only follow courses in the evening have other commitments which may affect their ability to continue studying. For this reason, some have commented on the strong commitment and motivation of those who complete courses of part-time study. Bourner and Hamed (1987a,b) found that degree entrants with qualifications that had been obtained through part-time study obtained better results than those with entry qualifications normally obtained as a result of full-time study.

Student Characteristics

A question that arises from any study of non-completion is whether some groups of students are more likely than others to withdraw early from courses, and, particularly, whether mature students, as opposed to the traditional further and higher education cohorts, are more at risk. This question has an added urgency at a time when questions are being raised about the impact of wider and more flexible entry procedures on standards in further and higher education.

Age

Woodley (1984) has referred to the relationship between age and performance as complex. This is borne out by the evidence reviewed for this study, which is generally inconclusive.

A number of studies have concluded that mature students in higher education are slightly (estimates vary between 4 per cent and

8 per cent) more likely than standard-aged students to leave a course of study early, although the performance of those who complete is generally as good if not better than that of standard-aged students.

An analysis of data on all undergraduates who entered British universities in 1972, 1973 and 1974 revealed that 17 per cent of the mature students did not successfully complete their courses compared with 13 per cent of younger students. Those over 50 were slightly less likely to complete their degree courses, but there was relatively little variation between the other age groups. Those aged 26–30 gained the best degrees and outperformed students aged under 21. After 30, however, 'degree perfomance declined with age' (Woodley, 1984; Woodley *et al.*, 1987).

In its analysis of first-year full-time and sandwich degree students in polytechnics and colleges, the DES (1992) found a bigger gap between mature and standard-age students: after standardising for sex, subject and entrance qualifications, the analysis showed that students aged 21 or less on entry had a leaving rate of 12 per cent compared with 19 per cent for older students.

A more recent report by the CVCP (quoted in the *Times Higher*, 19 January 1996) also indicates that mature students are more likely than younger ones to leave courses before completion. According to the report, students aged over 21 make up about 33 per cent of full-time home undergraduate students but about 40 per cent of non-completers.

Some institutional studies have produced a similar picture. In a study at Lancaster University, Lucas and Ward (1985) found that mature students were 'slightly more' likely than standard aged entrants to interrupt their studies or withdraw.

Research at the University of Exeter cited by Benn (1994) revealed that for the cohorts who entered between 1986/87 and 1989/90, there was a significant difference in withdrawal rates between mature students (16 per cent) and all students (8 per cent), although mature students were nearly as successful as the whole cohort in gaining good degrees.

Although there do not appear to have been many similar analyses in further education, a few studies also suggest that there has been some difference between mature and younger students in their rates of retention. Underwood's study (1974) in Birmingham found that further education students aged over 45, especially those who had left school at the minimum leaving age, were less likely to stay on the course. A report for BTEC (Smith and Bailey, 1993) found that students aged 20 or below at the time of registration were more likely to complete an award than those aged over 21, with the gap higher on full-time diploma programmes than on part-time certificate programmes.

The findings are not unanimous, however, and some recent studies reveal a different picture. At Wirral Metropolitan College, over 50 per cent of early leavers in 1993/94 were aged 25-plus. However, the college student body is largely made up of mature students and younger students seem more likely to leave in proportion to their numbers at the college. In 1993/94, the 18 and under age-group accounted for 14 per cent of enrolments but 23 per cent of early leavers, whereas the 19-plus group accounts for 86 per cent of enrolments but 77 per cent of early leavers (Wirral Metropolitan College, 1994).

Research at some universities has also found that mature learners are slightly *less* likely to withdraw than younger students:

> *'In three of the Schools and most strikingly in science, fewer mature students withdrew than one would have expected, other factors being equal. The situation in the fourth School is complicated by the very high proportion of withdrawals from franchised courses in this School. Franchised courses tend to have a higher proportion of mature students than courses taught on site; the percentage of mature students withdrawn from this School may reflect this rather than being connected to age at entry' (Moore, 1995: 14).*

> *'In none of the departments we visited were drop-out rates among non-standard students seen as exceptional. In one, in-house research found that in the second year, 60 per cent of younger students were still considering leaving compared with 19 per cent of mature students' (Bargh et al., 1994).*

In adult education, several investigations have found that younger students are more likely than older ones to leave courses before completion. A study of adult classes at Luton College of Higher Education (Hibbett, 1986) suggested that increasing age meant increased likelihood of completing. Similarly, Hamblin (1990) found the highest percentage of withdrawals among those aged 16–18 and the lowest among those aged 40–60. At the Open University it has been found that students aged 25–39 fare best, with 'drop-out' highest at the higher and lower end of the age-range, although students aged 60–64 were found to be particularly successful (Woodley and Parlett, 1983). In the 1994 MORI poll conducted for NIACE, younger people were considerably more likely to admit to giving up courses than older age groups.

Gender

Gender differences in completion rates and performance have been reported in all sectors. The study conducted by BTEC (Smith and Bailey, 1993) concluded that women were more likely to complete

This analysis was borne out by the information supplied by several AVAs for this project (although it was clear that in virtually all of them, women compose the majority of students).

Some evidence conflicts with the general finding. In their study of adult education classes at Luton College of Higher Education, Roberts and Webb (1979) found that all-male classes had lowest withdrawal rates of 9.8 per cent, while all-female classes had a rate of 12.6 per cent: 65 per cent of early leavers were women. This study was based on a small sample, however, and does not reflect the generality of the other evidence available.

Previous Qualifications

Some analyses have found a correlation between exit rates and low qualifications, but again the evidence is contradictory. Both Payne (1995) and the Audit Commission (1993), for example, found a relation between low GCSE scores and non-completion on A-level courses. Payne also found that students from less favoured socio-economic groups were the most likely not to complete A-level courses.

In higher education, the DES (1992) analysis of exit rates indicated that first degree full-time and sandwich students with three or more A-levels had slightly lower exit rates than those with two A-levels; however, the exit rate for those with only one A-level was lower still. Students entering with an ONC/HND qualification had substantially higher exit rates in almost every subject (Table 5).

Table 5. *Numbers of students by entry qualification and associated exit rates.*

	Number of beginners	Exit rate	Of which academic failure
Higher education	992	20%	6%
3 GCE A-levels	22,059	14%	4%
2 GCE A-levels	17,511	16%	5%
1 GCE A-level	1,687	11%	2%
OND, ONC	1,612	25%	10%
Other	11,569	18%	5%
Undefined	695	4%	-

Source: DES Statistical Bulletin 9/92.

Woodley *et al.* (1987) also came to the conclusion that those who entered universities on the basis of GCE A-levels were the most likely to gain a degree, irrespective of age:

> *'The figures for younger students were very similar to those for mature students within most of the entry qualification categories. The two major differences were that among students with foreign qualifications the younger students were much less likely to obtain a good degree, and among students with ONCs and HNCs, the younger students were somewhat less likely to gain any form of degree' (Woodley et al., 1987: 152).*

The CNAA (the Council for National Academic Awards) (1992) similarly found that the highest non-completion rates were among 'non-traditional' entrants and those with lowest formal qualifications, while in a national survey of the progress and performance of part-time Diploma in Management Studies students, Bord (1988) concluded that early leavers were 'slightly less qualified' than completers.

Institutional studies largely reflect the national findings. Roderick, Bell and Hamilton (1982) found high failure and drop-out rates among unqualified students at Sheffield University, particularly in the first term. Similarly, Woodley and Parlett (1983) found a correlation between withdrawal and low previous educational attainment at the Open University:

> *'Generally speaking, the lower a person's previous educational qualifications, the more likely he or she is to drop out.'*

More recently, Metcalfe and Halstead (1994) reported that OU foundation students without previous educational qualifications and those without professional qualifications below A-level have a higher rate of withdrawal than students with A-level qualifications or above. The Open University, West Midlands Region (1995) has found that students aged 40–60 with minimal prior educational attainment were proportionately more at risk.

As with the other variables discussed, not all studies reflect this finding and some have revealed the opposite. A study by the National Extension College, for example, found that the higher the qualification, the greater the likelihood of non-completion:

> *'Whereas it might have been expected that those with low educational qualifications were at risk of not completing courses, the opposite is true: the highest rate of giving up is among those who already have university degrees; the lowest rate is among those with GCE A-levels, followed by those with no previous educational qualifications' (NEC, 1991).*

In such cases, it is possible that people without qualifications who perceive a need for them may be more highly motivated than those who already have qualifications. This is borne out by the findings of some studies. The DES (1992) found that full-time and sandwich first degree students with existing higher education qualifications had higher than average exit rates. Benn (1994) also found that leavers from part-time certificated courses for adults at the University of Exeter were likely to be well qualified: 'the certificate was never the main reason for attending'. Similarly, Woodley and Parlett (1983) observed that, once a certain qualification level is achieved, motivation and retention can wane:

> *'In general, the more credits held by students at the beginning of the year, the greater appear their chances of being successful in that year. However, once an Ordinary degree (six credits) has been obtained, this trend is reversed. Those proceeding directly to an Honours degree (eight credits) have a very high wastage rate, and even those approaching Honours have only moderate success rates.'*

Many studies have also indicated that low qualifications on entry are not predictors of poor performance. From their research into entry qualifications and degree performance in the polytechnic sector in 1983, Bourner and Hamed (1987a) concluded that non-standard entrants had the highest percentage of good degrees, followed by those qualified at BTEC National level, HND/HNC level entrants and A-level entrants. They concluded that the correlation between A-level and degree performance was especially weak for those studying degree subjects which were not a continuation of pre-A-level subjects, and for those at the lower end of the range of A-level grades.

A study at Plymouth University has revealed that mature students (over 25) who entered with no qualifications or qualifications other than A-levels, gain the best degree results (*Times Higher*, 22 December 1995).

Some analysts have suggested that the relationship between performance and previous educational attainment is complicated by factors such as the form of previous study and the length of time since it was undertaken:

> *'It may be the recency of the prior educational experience that is most likely to affect withdrawal rates and that the more distant the entry qualification the higher the chance of drop-out' (CNAA 1992).*

> *'(For mature students) the link between school results and college or university performance is tenuous. Students may have several, sometimes many, intervening years between leaving and commencing their course. In that time a rich variety of experience may have contributed to their ability to tackle a college*

course. *On the other hand, some mature entrants leave school early and their subsequent experiences provide little preparation for academic study' (Kember, 1995: 72).*

Munn, MacDonald and Lowden (1992) were also unable to find a clear correlation between the entry qualifications possessed by students taking science, mathematics and engineering in further and higher education and their subsequent performance. They contend that entry qualifications tell us little either about the specific knowledge learned or the depth of understanding gained.

Opinions differ on the retention and performance of mature and standard-aged students in subject areas that are prone to high non-completion rates. Walker (1975) found little difference between the performance of mature students and standard students in the science faculties at the University of Lancaster. Mason (1989), however, concluded that even where mature students enter university through traditional routes, they are consistently outperformed in science and engineering by younger students. Some researchers suggest that this could be the result of a break in study (Walker, 1975). Woodley (1984), however, suggests that age also plays a part:

> '*Beyond age 30, experience seems to be cancelled out by increased learning difficulties and loss of study skills. The capacity for learning decreases perhaps by loss of memory and mental flexibility required to adapt to new perspectives. It appears that increased life expectancy does not compensate for the decline on maths and scientific skills resulting from a break in study.'*

In a later study, Woodley *et al.* argue that a combination of variables could account for the high rate of withdrawal among mature students in specific subject areas:

> '*It may be the case that (performance) figures reflect genuine subject differences, in that the greater life experience of older students may confer advantages in arts and social science, whereas it does not compensate for the lack of mathematical skills in the science area. However, it may be that different types of mature student are attracted to science subjects and one would need to look at their composition in terms of sex, age, educational qualifications and other variables.*
> *The drop-out rate on a given course will depend upon both the student population attracted and the nature of the course itself' (Woodley et al., 1987: 164).*

Other researchers propose that the admissions process has a bearing on differential completion rates between subjects. A report from South Bank University (Payne and Storan, 1995) points out that 'old' universities recruit most of their students during the first part of the calendar year, whereas many 'new' institutions rely largely on the 'Clearing' mechanism in August and September to fill places, especially in science and engineering. Clearing, as a number of studies have pointed out, is generally associated with high wastage rates, particularly in the first term or semester.

Different Student Cohorts

Unemployed students

It has been widely found that withdrawal rates in all sectors are particularly high among unemployed adults (Woodley and Parlett, 1983; Mansell and Parkin, 1990). The NIACE MORI poll (1994) indicated that those unemployed for five or more months are particularly likely to leave a course before completion (43 per cent).

Individual institutional studies reflect this finding: a survey of unwaged and unemployed students taking advantage of the 'Open Door' scheme to widen access for unwaged adults at GLOSCAT (Gloucestershire College of Arts and Technology) in 1988 showed that 42 per cent withdrew completely (Dekker and Whitfield, 1988). An FEU project at Stockton-Billingham College also found high drop-out rates among unemployed adults.

This phenomenon is widely attributed to financial factors such as benefit problems, the Availability for Work rule and finding employment. The level of completion is not high, however, even for those on government training schemes. Figures available on the results of the 'Training for Work' programme indicate that up to Summer 1994, a maximum of about 66 per cent 'completed an agreed programme of training'. 1995 figures show that only four out of 10 trainees completed the training with a national vocational qualification (*Times Higher*, 22 September 1995).

People with financial problems

In further education, mature student groups on low incomes tend to have high withdrawal rates. Wirral Metropolitan College (1993) identified the unemployed, single parents on benefits, adults in unskilled jobs, those vulnerable to redundancy, students with unemployed partners, students with dependent children and Wirral Task Force residents as groups with a relatively high rate of withdrawal from courses on main college sites. The college found that students receiving full remission were less likely to leave a course than those paying their own fees, a finding that disproves 'the assertion that fee remitted students enrol on courses without the same commitment to complete them'.

The Open University has also reported high wastage rates among the unemployed, students in manual occupations, the retired and those in institutions such as prisons and hospitals.

Ethnic minority groups

There appear to have been few studies of differences in retention and withdrawal rates between ethnic groups. However, there is one which has been cited by Metcalf (1993) – Singh's (1990) study of 1,533 degree entrants in five institutions. This found that withdrawal and success rates varied according to ethnic background. He concluded that Afro Caribbean students had the highest withdrawal rate through non-attendance or withdrawal (15 per cent) compared with white British (4 per cent) and Asian (2 per cent). Singh suggests this was probably connected with the fact that twice as many of the Afro Caribbean students in the research sample were non-standard entrants and 45 per cent were over 21.

A second study by Singh (of DipHE students at Bradford and Ilkley Community College) found that ethnic minority (mainly Asian) students had a higher early leaving rate than other students (35 per cent as against 28 per cent). There were also some racial and gender differences in performance: a higher proportion of ethnic minority than white men passed examinations, but white women had a pass rate of 68 per cent compared with 56 per cent among women from ethnic minorities. For those with standard entry qualifications, the pass rate was higher among ethnic minorities than among whites (75 per cent and 70 per cent). However, among non-standard entrants, ethnic minority students had a pass rate of 57 per cent compared with 68 per cent for white students.

Singh hypothesised that some Asians performed less well because of language difficulties (many were educated initially in the Indian sub-continent), for he found that there was an improvement in pass rates among later intakes who had been educated in Britain.

Access students

It is easier to find data on Access students than on other mature student cohorts. Information collected by the Access Validation Agencies is one of the few sources of data exclusively on mature students.

As in other areas of post-compulsory education, there is a view that progression and completion rates among Access students

Some studies have concluded that students with certain characteristics are more likely to leave a course than others. According to the DES (1992), for example, older students, male students and those with existing higher education qualifications were more likely than others to leave first degree courses in the polytechnic and college sector.

However, of the factors the DES (1992) found significant in non-completion – age, gender, subject studied and qualification on entry – there are only two on which the findings are broadly consistent: subject studied and gender. It has often been found that among mature students, males and students studying science and technology subjects are more susceptible to non-completion than female students and those studying arts, social sciences and vocational subjects:

> *'The present data do suggest that women are much less likely to experience academic problems and that maturity does not convey any advantage on science courses' (Woodley et al., 1987: 161).*

Kember (1995), however, warns that, when samples are large, statistically significant differences can result from very small discrepancies in retention rates.

The findings on age and previous qualifications are too diverse to be conclusive. Although there is some evidence that, until comparatively recently, mature students were slightly more likely than younger ones to leave a course before completion, some recent research reports cited earlier suggest that this may no longer be the case. The reasons for this could be to do with finance, accommodation and larger numbers of school leavers staying in full-time education.

Similarly, while some studies have found a higher withdrawal rate among students with low or non-standard qualifications on entry, others have not, and there is a widespread view that qualifications on entry to a degree programme are *not* a good predictor of withdrawal:

> *'No simple relation between the level of non-A-level entry qualifications and degree results is apparent' (Bourner and Hamed, 1987a).*

> *'The students most likely to leave without a qualification cannot be predicted prior to university entrance with any acceptable degree of certainty' (Taylor and Johnes, 1989).*

> *'The degree of certainty with which potential non-graduates can be predicted is small. School examination results are not as successful as university examination results in predicting the incidence of non-completion' (Johnes, 1990).*

> '*A low level of entry qualification does not indicate withdrawal and an open access policy does not seem to contribute to the attrition rate*' (Benn, 1994).

The diversity of research findings on the possible links between student characteristics and drop-out suggests that it would be very unsafe to use the former as predictors of non-completion. Kember (1995) argues that such a process would be of dubious value:

> '*Early research on entry characteristics which correlated with drop-out ... served only to confirm that there is not a single explanation or cure for drop-out ... It is comforting that entry characteristics are such poor predictors of success. Students with the wrong initial data set are not pre-destined to fail, however hard they try. The faculty and the college do have a role to play in determining the success or otherwise of their students*' (Kember, 1995: 32).

Kember makes the additional point that the factors associated with high withdrawal do not necessarily cause it and should not therefore be used in any facile strategy to prevent non-completion:

> '*Statistical relationships do not imply causation. It may be true that drop-out is highest in the first year of a course but it is clearly ludicrous to suppose that admitting students directly to the second year is going to reduce drop-out. Similarly, it may be true that engineering courses have higher drop-out rates than arts ones, but forcing students into arts courses may actually increase attrition, as most students would end up in courses in which they had no interest*' (Kember, 1995: 70).

Entry characteristics and subject choice cannot, by themselves, account for non-completion and many have argued that it is more helpful to focus on what happens to students *after* enrolment than on predicting success at entry.

The reasons for non-completion, other than academic failure, will be explored in the next chapter.

Part 2
What Do We Know About the Reasons for
Non-Completion?

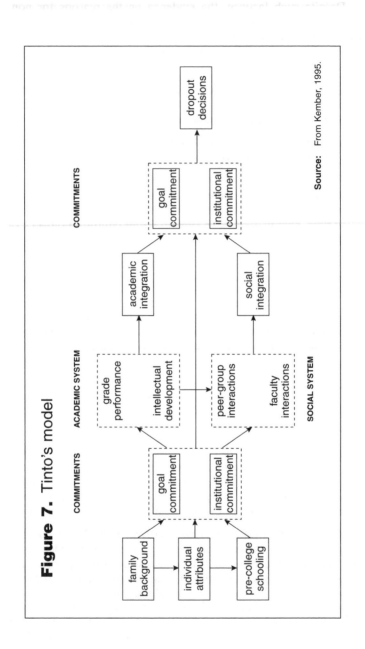

Figure 7. Tinto's model

Source: From Kember, 1995.

impact on their goals and institutional commitment. Kember claims that the testing of this model by a number of researchers has confirmed its validity, although some have found that factors external to the institution play a greater role in student drop-out than the model suggests. Another critique is that Tinto's model is based on the traditional full-time, campus-based, younger student and therefore has less relevance for mature students involved in different modes of study. Despite these limitations, the evidence on student non-completion suggests that Tinto's model still has considerable relevance.

Adult General Education Students

The reasons for withdrawal vary according to type of institution and type of study. Hibbett (1986) found the reasons given by those who left recreational courses offered by a college of higher education mainly involved dissatisfaction with the course itself, whereas students on award-bearing courses tended to give reasons that were more associated with outside commitments and academic problems. Little dissatisfaction was expressed with content and arrangements.

In a study of local authority provision, Herrick (1986) also found that the reasons given for leaving non-vocational classes were largely course-related (45 per cent), with others citing external, particularly work related reasons.

A more recent investigation (Beddow, 1994) found that the majority of withdrawals from adult evening courses at a tertiary college had been for external, personal reasons. However, the researcher suggests that institutional expectations and practices could also contribute to non-completion:

> *'Tutors noted the problem of expecting high drop-out rates leading to over-large groups which contribute to and therefore perpetuate high drop-out rates' (Beddow, 1994: 14).*

A number of studies (e.g. Cullen, 1994) show that a significant cause of non-completion among those who have been obliged to interrupt learning because of illness or other factors, is the fear of not being able to catch up on the academic work and regain a sense of belonging to the course. Wilkinson (1982) found that permanent drop out was often caused by apprehension at returning to study after losing continuity. Likewise, a study of withdrawal from modem foreign language classes revealed that the:

> *'single most common factor, cited by 90 per cent, was fear of not being able to advance with the rest of class having missed more than one lesson (although staff took pains to ensure that*

a revision element was built into their lesson plans)' (Netword News, undated).

Adult Basic Education Students

Data from adult basic education projects in Cheshire showed the main reasons for withdrawal to be evenly divided between personal and institutional factors. The following mixture of reasons were cited for leaving one-to-one support:

* had progressed as far as was possible
* tutor leaving
* tutor attitudes
* lack of progress and confidence
* work boring or not pitched at right level
* work-related reasons
* domestic problems.

The investigation suggested that any change in one-to-one arrangements could have a detrimental effect on student commitment (Sanders, 1977).

In another study of adult basic education students (Clarke, 1989), the reasons given for leaving were predominantly outside pressures such as work-related reasons, care of dependants, housing problems. Less often quoted reasons related to course arrangements, personal progress and loss of motivation.

Distance Learning Students

A study by the National Extension College (1991) indicated that the main factors influencing decisions to give up studying were outside pressures: limited time for study, employment and family or domestic pressures. Less frequently expressed reasons were health problems and course considered unsuitable or too difficult.

The survey also indicated that the reasons varied according to student characteristics: health problems and domestic pressures were cited far more frequently by those without employment than those with; respondents without educational qualifications were far more likely to cite pressures at work as reasons for giving up than those who had studied up to at least A-level. However, those with A-levels had been more likely to choose a course that did not provide the content they really wanted. The study revealed little criticism about the content of courses and it is suggested that this might have been because they felt inhibited about criticism which might imply that they were unable to cope (NEC, 1991).

Further Education Students

Most of the national evidence available on the reasons for non-completion refers to all students or standard (16–19) aged students. The former Further Education Unit (1994) refers to inadequacies in areas such as pre-course contact, induction, classroom experience and the college environment as the factors which cause many students to leave courses. However, the Audit Commission's (1993) survey of 16–19-year-olds on full-time courses indicated that financial hardship, inappropriate course choice and deficits in core skills areas contributed significantly to non-completion of further education courses among this age group. A different conclusion was reached in the BTEC study of 2,000 students on full- and part-time programmes (Smith and Bailey, 1993). This attributed the loss of 31 per cent of students on part-time certificate programmes and 19 per cent of those on full-time diploma programmes largely to employment-related factors:

> *'Getting a job is one of the main reasons for fill-time students leaving programmes before achieving the relevant award. Loss or change of employment and other work-related factors are among main reasons why part-time students leave early' (Smith and Bailey, 1993).*

Other causes cited in the BTEC report are programme-related, academic (poor grades or assessment achievement), and personal: family, health or financial reasons.

Some colleges have conducted in-house studies of the reasons for leaving courses. Wirral Metropolitan College (1993 and 1994) has found that the reasons cited by former students at the end of 1992 were predominantly personal and financial, followed by institutional and course-related reasons. The reasons for students withdrawing from courses in 1993/94 were largely classified as unknown (40 per cent). The other reasons were, in order of frequency:

- personal/other (23 per cent)
- transfer (10 per cent)
- dissatisfaction with course (10 per cent).

Research at the college has suggested that financial problems play a particularly large part in influencing decisions to withdraw:

> *'Students who were experiencing financial difficulties were twice as likely to drop out and students who were worse off than they expected to be were even more likely to drop out.'*

The groups most likely to leave for financial reasons were identified as single parents, students with unemployed partners, students with dependent children, those living in Wirral Task Force area and students receiving local authority grants. Employer-sponsored students experienced fewest financial problems (Wirral Metropolitan College, 1993).

Other colleges also cite financial problems as a major factor leading to mature student withdrawal. A student counsellor at a college which responded to this project claimed that 90 per cent of the people he sees who subsequently leave a course of study have financial problems:

> 'If they are also finding a course difficult and are not aware of a suitable alternative, there is a strong likelihood that people for whom finance is a problem will leave.'

In a survey of a small sample of full-time students, the majority aged over 21, at Kensington and Chelsea College, 60 per cent claimed to have considered leaving courses because of financial factors; 19 per cent had considered leaving for course or academic-related reasons (including transfer); and 8 per cent for personal reasons (Kensington and Chelsea College, 1995).

Another college found that non-completion of vocational courses is linked to current occupational status. Interviews with a small sample of students who had failed to complete the off-course work required to gain Stage 1 of the City and Guilds Further and Adult Education Teachers Certificate suggested that non-completion was: 'significantly related to teacher status: far more current teachers than non-teachers completed'. The reasons cited for non-completion related mainly to job and personal circumstances. However, according to the researcher, these tended to camouflage more deep-rooted problems such as lack of confidence in ability to cope with the demands of the course. Moreover, it is suggested that loss of contact with the college after classes were completed may have been a major factor in non-completion of the assignments:

> 'The course offers students the possibility of completing up to three years after the end of class time. A significant factor that completers had in common was that most completed within four months and/or had continuing close links with the college. It seems that the longer completion is left the harder it becomes' (Harvey, 1995b).

Part-Time Further Education Students

A survey of over 100 part-time students, the majority aged over 25, at Kensington and Chelsea College showed that nearly 80 per cent had considered not continuing because of personal circumstances, course-related reasons and dislike of going out in the evenings.

Over a third also found it difficult to work from home and found finance a problem (Kensington and Chelsea College, 1995).

Research at another college revealed that institutional and academic reasons combined with time pressures led two-thirds of a sample of over 500 part-time students to withdraw from their programmes of study (Mansell and Parkin, 1990). The study suggested that the following institutional factors also contributed to student dissatisfaction:

1. Enrolment experience: over half said they were not informed about what their course entailed before they enrolled, and would like more guidance. Most had not seen their future teacher at enrolment.

2. Classroom experience: about a third reacted negatively to their classroom experience, e.g. pace too fast and determined by the teacher.

3. Advice, guidance and academic counselling: students complained that they had not had enough time to discuss problems related to their study. Nearly half found the college impersonal and few were aware of counselling or sports facilities.

4. Time pressures: combining part-time study and full-time employment posed serious difficulties.

5. Lack of study skills: few of the sample had undertaken any previous related study.

Unemployed Students

A Further Education Unit project at Stockton-Billingham College found that the reasons for leaving courses given by 60 per cent of unemployed students were largely related to dissatisfaction with courses, teaching method and learning modes.

A study of unemployed adults who had withdrawn from courses at a further education college in Gloucestershire found that dissatisfaction with the course was also important: 22.5 per cent considered the course unsuitable or had underestimated its demands. However, the main reason for leaving a course was finding employment (40 per cent). Additional reasons cited were childcare problems, personal or health factors and financial problems (Dekker and Whitfield, 1989) (Figures 8 and 9).

According to this study, the problems experienced by unemployed students while studying were predominantly financial (69 per cent), with the costs of examination fees, books and childcare mentioned.

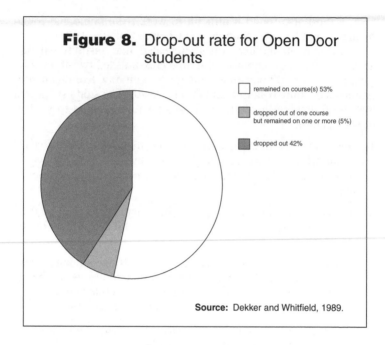

Figure 8. Drop-out rate for Open Door students

remained on course(s) 53%

dropped out of one course but remained on one or more (5%)

dropped out 42%

Source: Dekker and Whitfield, 1989.

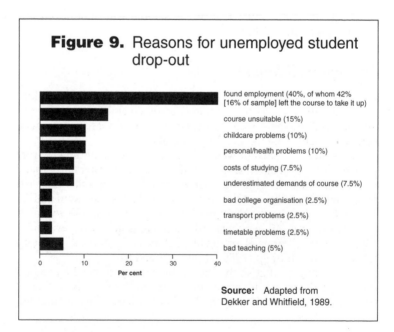

Figure 9. Reasons for unemployed student drop-out

found employment (40%, of whom 42% [16% of sample] left the course to take it up)

course unsuitable (15%)

childcare problems (10%)

personal/health problems (10%)

costs of studying (7.5%)

underestimated demands of course (7.5%)

bad college organisation (2.5%)

transport problems (2.5%)

timetable problems (2.5%)

bad teaching (5%)

Per cent

Source: Adapted from Dekker and Whitfield, 1989.

Transport problems affected those in rural areas more than others and largely concerned cost, availability and convenience. It is significant that two-thirds of those with transport problems withdrew from their courses.

Access Students

While some access consortia record total withdrawal rates from member institutions they have not all yet gathered reasons centrally.

The reasons for withdrawal quoted in reports provided by several AVAs for this enquiry stressed the role, in decisions to withdraw, of outside pressures such as personal and family commitments, childcare and, particularly, problems with finance:

> *'Financial difficulties were the most often quoted reason for non-completion.'*

> *'Childcare and finance remain difficulties across the Consortium. All tutors reported on difficult financial situations for many students. In some cases, there were reports of real poverty.'*

> *'The main reason for the high number of withdrawals appears to be financial difficulties or changes in circumstances. Some students succeeded in finding employment, others were demotivated by unsuccessful applications to HE and left their Access course in the spring term. The cuts in students grants and the DSS regulations on the 21-hour rule may also be factors.'*

> *'In June 1994, 34 per cent left courses early, an increase of 12 per cent over the previous year. Twenty-five per cent left for personal reasons – family, finance and work pressures and 12 per cent left to take up employment.'*

> *'We have not been able to collect comprehensive data on the reasons for withdrawal but informal feedback suggests that common causes are primarily domestic or employment-related: moving out of the area, getting a job, changing job, family commitments. Anecdotal evidence suggests that only a small proportion withdraw for academic reasons.'*

Other AVA reports have identified academic problems as important factors in withdrawal. In one Access Federation where study skills and Mathematics are compulsory elements of courses, a large number of students dropped out within the first few weeks of the commencement of the course. One of the main reasons was thought to be:

> *'the difficulties which many students experience when they are confronted with studies in maths for the first time in many years.'*

Other reports suggest that some non-completing students are unprepared for the demands of Access courses:

> *'Some appeared to lose interest in the course because they had unreal expectations of what was demanded of them.'*

In her case study of discontinuing Access students, Cullen (1994) also found that respondents had underestimated the time needed to cope with the workload.

Higher Education Students

Most studies of withdrawal from higher education courses have identified a mix of personal and institutional reasons for student non-completion. Johnes' (1990) analysis of data for the whole undergraduate cohort that entered higher education in 1979 indicated that the reasons for non-graduation were largely academic (42 per cent), personal (37 per cent), and course or institution transfer (20 per cent).

The CVCP survey of student financial support in 1995 revealed that departures due to academic failure rose by 20 per cent that year compared with a 5 per cent increase in withdrawals for non-academic reasons. However, taken as a whole, CVCP surveys since 1991/92 indicate that withdrawals for academic and non-academic reasons have grown at a roughly comparable rate over that period (*Times Higher*, 19 January 1996).

Non-academic reasons

Many research studies have found that mature students tend to cite non-academic factors as the main cause of their withdrawal. For example, in a study of entrants to Lancaster University, Lucas and Ward (1985) found that mature students were interrupting their studies or withdrawing mainly for personal or financial reasons.

The Woodley *et al.* (1987) analysis of data from the Universities Statistical Record indicated that 7 per cent of mature students left university without degrees in 1972, 1973 and 1974 because they failed academically, and a further 10 per cent withdrew for non-academic reasons – the majority in the (vague) 'other reasons' category (Woodley *et al.*, 1987: 161).

Outside pressures have been cited as the main reasons for withdrawing from Open University courses. A survey of students who had not completed final registration revealed that the reasons given were overwhelmingly related to domestic and work circumstances (77 per cent). Only 21 per cent referred to study problems caused by the form and content of the courses (cited in Woodley *et al.*, 1987).

Similar findings emerged from later Open University surveys: one of students who had left third-level mathematics courses (cited in Woodley *et al.*, 1987), and another of 'dormant OU students' – registered undergraduates not currently taking courses but entitled to re-enter the system at any time (Woodley, 1992). In both cases, domestic and employment factors emerged as paramount. The second study indicated that many 'dormant' students had decided that another course elsewhere was more suited to their needs and circumstances, and that others were prevented from continuing by factors such as the cost of study, the summer school attendance requirement or illness. Those with low qualifications and those who had not gained any course credit were more likely to have experienced such barriers. Dissatisfaction with the Open University was not generally a significant factor, although 17 per cent of the group without credit were not happy with the OU teaching system or staff.

Hand, Gambles and Cooper (1994) identified changes in personal circumstances to do with home, family, employment or finance as the most significant reasons for adult learner withdrawal in post-compulsory learning systems. Several of the other reasons which they identify are also more specific to adult learners, for example problems with benefits and with the Availability for Work and 21-hour rules, or withdrawal of financial support for study (e.g. from employers).

Personal factors also dominate the reasons for leaving accelerated and intensive degree courses. Foong *et al.* (1994) found that the causes expressed for withdrawal were more to do with financial, personal, health and stress problems than with academic pressures.

A study in Scotland also found that personal problems such as finance, childcare, family commitments and other time commitments were important factors associated with mature student non-completion in further and higher education (Munn, MacDonald and Lowden, 1992).

Non-academic reasons for non-completion appear to be growing among the whole student population. For example, an analysis of withdrawal from courses at Liverpool John Moores University in 1992/93 (LJMU, 1995b) revealed that personal factors had significantly affected the decisions to leave of over 60 per cent of both part-time and full-time former students.

A survey by the CVCP suggests that in recent years, student with-drawal for non-academic reasons has been increasing faster than the growth in student numbers:

'Of the 40,000 students who left university courses during 1992/93, 15,000 did so because of academic failure – an

increase of 15 per cent compared with the previous year, and 25,000 left for other reasons: a growth of 30 per cent compared with the previous year or about twice the rate of the increase in student numbers (which was about 15 per cent). Complete data for 1993/94 is not yet available, but the indications are that the growth in students leaving for reasons other than examination failure has continued to increase' (CVCP press release, 28 June 1995).

Financial problems

Financial problems following the freezing of Local Authority awards and the removal of student eligibility for benefits have been widely identified as a major cause of student withdrawal.

The *Push Guide to Which University 1995* proposed three main non-academic reasons why students are failing to complete their courses: accommodation problems (exacerbated by the increased number of undergraduates), money problems and social factors.

A survey by the National Union of Students and the National Westminster Bank discovered that one in five undergraduates had considered dropping out because of money worries (*Times Educational Supplement*, 19 August 1994). Some studies indicate that mature students are particularly vulnerable. One article quoted a student finance survey showing that the average level of debt increased considerably with the age of a student: from £2,476 for those aged 17–21 to £6,105 for those aged over 26 (*Education*, 8 July 1994).

A survey of adult students on an applied social science course at Ruskin College between 1981 and 1986 (most of them self-, LEA- or employer-financed) revealed that the proportion and scale of debt among students was increasing, with the main concerns housing and travel costs (Bryant and Noble, 1989).

Bargh *et al.* (1994) also refer to the financial difficulties experienced by 'non-standard' mature students, while the Liverpool John Moores study revealed that financial considerations had contributed to the withdrawal of over 95 per cent of former part-time mature students. Other studies, however, have found that financial problems were stressed more by former full-time than by former part-time students, partly because many of the latter remained in employment while studying.

The CVCP has acknowledged that financial difficulties may be partly responsible for the increase in withdrawal rates:

'It is not possible to calculate the contribution of financial hardship to a student's decision to leave a course, because of the interaction with other factors, (but) the increasing financial pressures on students from less well-off backgrounds as a result

of the reduction of means-tested grants, may aggravate other difficulties causing some students to leave their course' (CVCP press release, 28 June 1995).

The CVCP's survey of student financial support in 1995 indicates that there is a correlation between mature student drop-out and financial hardship. It shows that full-time undergraduates aged over 25 were responsible for 45 per cent of bids for support from access funds (*Times Higher*, 19 January 1996). Moore (1995), however, has concluded from her research at Sheffield Hallam University that the link between financial difficulties and student withdrawal is not as clear-cut as other commentators have assumed. She found that financial and accommodation problems were likely to be mentioned as secondary factors in supporting decisions to leave courses.

Course- and institution-related reasons

Moore found that course and institutional factors were the main reasons for withdrawal cited by former students. Over 40 per cent of those followed up stated that they had disliked or found the course unsuitable, while less than 20 per cent cited personal factors such as finance, accommodation, illness and employment. However, Moore cautions that personal reasons may be underestimated:

'Students may find it easier to say they left for course-related reasons rather than for personal reasons, and it may be the combination of dislike of course with other issues, such as not having settled in, that leads to withdrawal.'

The Sheffield Hallam study found that three factors were significantly associated with student withdrawal:

1. Frustrated expectations: 54 per cent of respondents reported that higher education had fallen short of their expectations. Often this related more to course content, level and teaching methods than to other factors.

2. Off-site courses: 'A strikingly large proportion – 33 per cent – of the withdrawn students had been studying off-site on franchise/foundation courses' (Moore, 1995: 14).

3. Entry through Clearing: 24 per cent of withdrawn students gave as their first reason for accepting a place at SHU the reason that it was the only place they could get at the grades achieved (*ibid.*, 16).

These factors have also been identified as significant in other studies. The study conducted at Liverpool John Moores University, for example, found that entering through the Clearing process could be a significant factor, since 44 per cent of the former full-time students covered by that study had entered through this route (LJMU, 1995b).

Other reports have also found off-site, franchised courses to be associated with high withdrawal rates, with problems such as lack of facilities and limited interaction with other higher education students frequently cited by former students:

> *'In some instances, further education franchises may be little more than "academic overspill estates" which provide little or none of the extra-curricular infrastructure of full undergraduate life ... where library and IT facilities are inadequate, and where a scholarly ethos is lacking' (Abramson, 1994).*

> *'The lack of a large contingent of fellow higher education students is seen as limiting the educational experience; it may be that HE students in a further education college feel the atmosphere as less "adult" ' (Brady and Metcalfe, 1994: 276).*

> *'Franchise students in some colleges felt culturally isolated from the reality of higher education' (Bird, Crawley and Sheibani, 1993).*

Moore (1995), however, stresses that off-site courses vary considerably and do not have a common identity, and the HEFCE (1995) concluded 'from the limited information available that there was no evidence that the quality or experience of higher education students in further education colleges was any better or worse than those of their counterparts in higher education institutions'.

Part-time HE students

The research literature suggests that part-time higher education students experience particular difficulties arising from the pressures involved in trying to combine study with outside commitments, particularly employment:

> *'The pressures produced by travel and all the other problems of fitting in part-time study alongside employment and/or other activities and responsibilities are, of course, considerable, far in excess of anything adolescent students have to face. Most part-time students freely admit to having seriously considered dropping out on at least one occasion and many do so' (Tight, 1987: 19–24).*

> *'Part-time students, especially those taking more than one course, experienced many competing demands on their time and particularly work pressures' (Munn, MacDonald and Lowder, 1992).*

The Liverpool John Moores study identified work commitments as a significant contributory factor in the case of 59 per cent of non-completing part-time students. Personal reasons such as family commitments, medical advice, maternity leave, childcare problems, changes in employment status and stresses experienced while studying were also mentioned (LJMU, 1995b).

Benn (1994) has also found that many adult learners left part-time programmes at the University of Exeter largely because of external pressures such as work, domestic and family commitments, and financial, health and transport problems. A significant number also said that courses did not live up to their expectations. About a third were unprepared for the work involved.

A national survey of the progress and performance of students taking a part-time Diploma in Management Studies produced a similar picture. The findings indicated that main reasons for early withdrawal were job-related (46 per cent); personal circumstances (22 per cent); dissatisfaction with the course (20 per cent) and academic reasons (13 per cent). The study showed that by the beginning of the second year, 18 per cent of students had left, 12 per cent of them in the first term because the course was considered unsuitable or did not meet expectations. Eleven per cent left during the second year (Bord, 1988).

The fact that courses were held in the evenings was identified as an important contributory factor in a survey of non-completing part-time students on first degree courses in the former polytechnic and college sector (Bourner *et al.*, 1991).

Like full-time students, therefore, part-time learners are likely to cite a mixture of non-academic and course-related reasons for leaving courses, with non-academic reasons frequently predominating. There are, however, variations according to institution, subject and student characteristics. As Metcalf (1993) asserts:

'The experience of students is likely to vary greatly between institutions, due to wide differences in culture, facilities and the mix of students.'

Some of these differences will be explored in Chapter 7.

Chapter 7

Variations and Common Findings

The evidence indicates that the reasons for withdrawal vary according to student group, the nature of the institution, the support available and the subject studied. More often than younger learners, mature students cite non-academic reasons for leaving a course. However, the stated reasons for withdrawal need to be treated with caution. There are usually a number of inter-related reasons for leaving a course and former students often cite those that are the most recent or which protect their self-esteem. Nevertheless, research has identified a number of common factors associated with non-completion.

Although there is some consistency in research and institutional findings, with many analyses finding that mature students tend to give non-academic reasons for leaving a programme of study, Woodley *et al.* (1987) point out that the stated reasons for withdrawal vary according to group and subject. From the evidence they analysed, they noted that the predominance of non-academic reasons for non-completion did not occur uniformly across all mature student groups: it was not true for men, for those taking science courses or for those entering higher education on the basis of ONCs and HNCs. For example, Woodley's earlier analysis of data on over 18,000 mature full-time or sandwich, first-degree students had revealed that whereas withdrawal from arts and social sciences was mainly for non-academic reasons, students were leaving science subjects mainly for reasons of academic failure (Woodley, 1984).

Cohort Differences

The evidence suggests that certain groups of students experience specific difficulties which can lead to their not continuing on a course. It has been noted, for example, that Access students often withdraw because of the contrast between the supportive environment of an Access courses and the less intimate and friendly atmosphere of a large and intimidating higher education institution:

> *'The most common reasons for intermitting were expressed as pressure caused by the different levels of tutor support between the Access course and the undergraduate programme, combined with the increased workload. There is a potential for culture clash for some students who come from a climate of intensive individual support on their Access courses' (University of Brighton, 1994: 3–4).*

> *'A number of former Access students commented on the differences between those courses and the University, saying that they found the University less friendly and felt they had less support from staff. One had difficulty with the contrast with her previous Access course where all the students were mature women, many with children. She found that they "pulled you through". On the degree course there were only two other mature students and she felt much more isolated' (Moore, 1995: 20).*

Individuals from minority ethnic groups and people with disabilities or special needs can also experience specific pressures and difficulties arising from lack of support, prejudice and discrimination which can lead to decisions to leave. While there is a scarcity of evidence on the experience of these groups (Metcalf, 1993), there is a growing body of evidence on the experience of women in education and the pressures that can lead to their withdrawal.

Gender Differences

Studies in all sectors have found significant differences between the sexes in their reported reasons for withdrawing from courses. As is to be expected, family commitments are cited by significantly more women than men, while men tend to stress course-, finance- and employment-related issues (Wirral Metropolitan College, 1994). This has been found in all types of provision, including distance learning:

> *'Gender had a significant impact on the reasons given. Family or domestic pressures were cited by more women than men; men claimed more often than women that the course content was not really what they wanted, and men more frequently gave limited time as a reason than women' (NEC, 1991).*

The DES analysis of leavers from first-year degree courses at colleges and polytechnics showed that men were more likely to leave for reasons of academic failure and women more likely to leave for personal and other non-academic reasons (Figure 10).

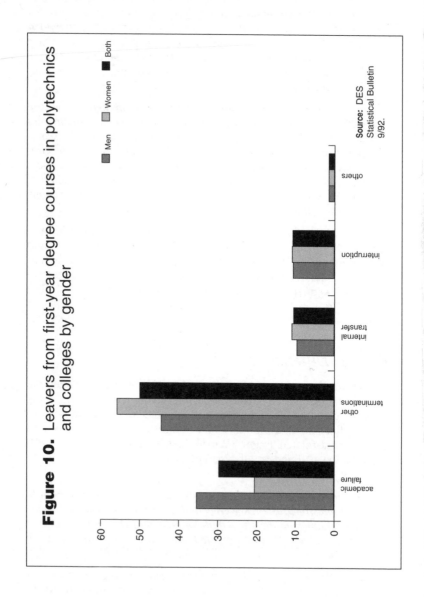

Figure 10. Leavers from first-year degree courses in polytechnics and colleges by gender

Source: DES Statistical Bulletin 9/92.

Combining domestic responsibilities with study is a common problem for women students and many studies indicate that providers often fail to take this into account. Foong *et al.* (1994), for example, comment on the extent to which lack or inadequacy of creche provision on accelerated and intensive programmes has affected women students, all of whom withdrew from one course. The majority of the second cohort of entrants (63 per cent) were also dissatisfied with the quality of creche facilities.

Hibbett (1986) found that 53 per cent of students who had left award-bearing courses at a college of higher education were married women. He concluded that this was probably the result of the conflict between domestic pressures and a demanding course. Cullen (1994) also refers to the pressure of 'juggling roles for women whose aims and purposes in life are so often discounted', while Metcalf (1993) cites a university study in Wales which found that mature women students expressed twice as many concerns as men.

Edwards' (1993) study of women in higher education has also demonstrated how difficult it can be for women to combine their family and student roles. Her research subjects found that their family life experience was neither valued nor academically acceptable within masculine-oriented education institutions and no account was taken of their domestic commitments. At the same time, many found it difficult to connect their educational life with their family lives, as male partners (and sometimes other relatives) felt it affected family relationships and interfered with the women's domestic and emotional commitments. Women who persisted in trying to connect the two 'greedy institutions' encountered problems. Sixteen of 31 interviewees reported verbal abuse and arguments and three physical violence.

Edwards observes that participation in higher education will continue to be difficult for women while they remain torn between these diverging pressures:

> *'While the policies and institutions concern themselves with inputs and outputs and privilege disciplines over students, and while the balance of male identity depends on a masculine/ feminine demarcation that associates loss of power with loss of identity, combining education with family life (and relations with men especially) will never be easy for women.'*

Munn, MacDonald and Lowden (1992) also reported that trying to combine education and family was a constant dilemma for mature women students. They found that students on advanced or full-time courses tended to organise their lives so that their family could fit in with their studying but that the success of this depended on having a supportive family or partner. A study of male student experience, however (Maynard and Pearsall, 1994), indicated that married male students tend to receive far more support and encouragement from their partners than married female students. Although the women in their study had virtually all deferred their entry to higher education until they were satisfied that their children no longer required their continuous presence in the home:

> *'their decision was contingent on the responses of partner and family to a much greater extent than was the case with the student fathers. If approval was not forthcoming from the partners of student mothers their relationship could be put under strain and even at risk. None of the married male students experienced such negative reactions ... Male students frequently benefited from a striking level of solidarity from their partners, despite difficult financial circumstances arising from the loss of the main income to the household.'*

Like the other studies cited, this one found that female students experience considerable stress when there is a clash between domestic and education commitments:

> *'We discovered how severe the pressure on female students could be, if their family expected them to maintain their role as manager of the home and pursue their studies simultaneously ... Most prioritised respectively the demands of the home and their courses as the pressures each presented varied. By contrast, the men were able to commit themselves more wholeheartedly to their student lives, academically and socially ... While both sexes experienced stress during their studies it was of a different nature and intensity for the women.'*

Thus a study which set out to investigate the problems experienced by male students threw into relief the far greater problems experienced by women. The researchers concluded:

> *'It is ironic that research into the experiences of male mature students should primarily reinforce the picture that has recently been emerging of the struggles of female students who have domestic obligations ... They are sometimes unnecessarily burdened by the lack of sympathy of their partners, friends and families, and, sadly, by the ignorance of many higher education institutions of their needs' (Maynard and Pearsall, 1994: 232–234).*

Many other reports have commented on the lack of support and opposition some women experience when they embark upon a serious programme of study. Green and Percy (1991) cite reports from Access courses on male partners' resistance to women's involvement, while Brady (1993) found that only about a quarter of the women on an Access programme in mathematics received any positive support from partners. In her study of non-completing Access students, Cullen (1994) found that a significant proportion of women students had experienced physical and/or verbal abuse from their partners or ex-partners while they were on the course.

This kind of evidence suggests that the reasons for leaving courses may be qualitatively different for mature students from those of standard age students.

Differences Between Mature and Younger Students

Metcalf (1993) found that few studies have examined the extent to which non-traditional student experience differs from that of standard students. There is, however, some evidence on the kind of problems that are commonly experienced by mature students.

Mature students are more likely than younger ones to enter higher education with no or 'non-standard' qualifications and with a gap since full-time study. It has been found that many consequently suffer from a sense of inadequacy about their perceived lack of academic skills. Roderick and Bell (1981), for example, found that major factors involved in the non-completion of unqualified mature students at the University of Sheffield were insecurity, lack of confidence, inability to cope with work, failure to keep up with course demands, poor study skills, deficiencies in note-taking and essay-writing and unrealistic expectations with regard to subject and institution.

Metcalf (1993) quotes a study at University College, North Wales which found that 32 per cent of mature students were worried about their ability to cope academically, even if they had entered with A-levels. She also refers to a study at Thames Polytechnic which revealed that although 90 per cent of mature students had standard level qualifications, over 25 per cent felt that their previous education was inadequate for the course. If such feelings are compounded by practical and personal problems, students may leave the course. As Roderick, Bell and Hamilton (1982) observed in relation to unqualified students at Sheffield University: 'surviving seemed to be their major concern and a proportion were not able to overcome the problems that faced them.'

As noted in Chapter 6, most analyses have also found that mature students are more likely than younger ones to leave courses for reasons that are external to the course or institution. This is true across the different sectors. As stated in the study by the Open University and Coventry University (Open University, West Midlands Region, 1995), non-completion has less to do with the institution than with 'the demands that life makes on adults'.

A study at Wirral Metropolitan College (1994) showed that personal and other reasons for leaving were more likely to be given by older students while younger students were more likely to leave for job-related reasons.

The Department of Education and Science found that the reasons for non-completion among mature undergraduates in the former polytechnic and colleges sector largely fell into the category of termination for personal reasons, employment, financial reasons, death and unknown reasons (55 per cent) (DES, 1992). Figure 11 shows that students aged 22-plus terminated study more often than younger students for non-academic reasons, while those aged 21 and under had a greater proportion of academic failures or internal transfers.

Similarly, although the Sheffield Hallam study (Moore, 1995) found that the most significant reasons for leaving were course-related, further analysis of the data undertaken specifically for this project by Rebecca Moore showed that there were some differences between older and younger students, notably the greater propensity of older students to cite personal and employment-related reasons for non-completion:

Primary reason	Age 18–20	Age 20-plus
	%	%
Course unsuitable/disliked	51	32
Personal and childcare	17	32
Academic problems	15	9
Finance	5	9
Accommodation	5	0
Illness	5	5
Offered work	0	14

The analysis also indicated that:

- the personal problems faced by younger students (typically homesickness and loneliness) were different from those cited by mature students: childcare problems, difficulties in shifting from a role as parent/housewife/worker to that of student: 'These could be seen as manifestations of a similar issue, i.e. negotiating a change in role and identity, which impacts on different age groups in different ways'
- mature students were less likely to find courses unsuitable

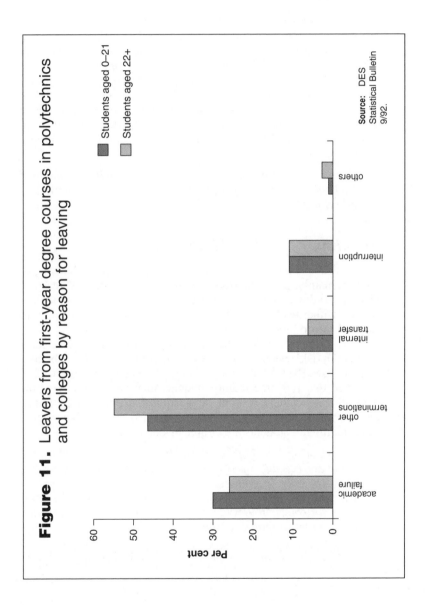

Figure 11. Leavers from first-year degree courses in polytechnics and colleges by reason for leaving

Students aged 0–21
Students aged 22+

Source: DES Statistical Bulletin 9/92.

- taking a job was more important for older students (Moore, 1995).

Several studies have also found that financial difficulties tend to be more acute among mature students. According to the DFE Student and Income Survey for 1992/93, this is because mature students have substantially higher levels of spending than younger students. As noted in Chapter 6, it is often financial pressures on top of other problems that leads to non-continuation. The CVCP survey of student financial support has indicated that full-time undergraduates aged over 25 account for 45 per cent of those applying for help from access funds (*Times Higher*, 19 January 1996), while Cullen's (1994) study revealed:

> *'how very hard it is to be a mature student with no financial backing in the form of a grant and no childcare provision or allowance.'*

Are Mature Students More at Risk?

There is substantial evidence, therefore, that mature students leave courses mainly, to quote Bord (1988), for 'facts of life' reasons. Herrick (1986) concludes that the totality of research on mature student withdrawal shows 'the vulnerability of adult education to external factors'.

This brings us back to the question of whether mature students are a 'high risk' category in terms of non-completion. Some believe that they are. The CVCP survey of student financial support in 1995 indicated that full-time mature students may be more susceptible than others and there is some suggestion that this may be linked to financial factors. Wagner (1990) has also argued that mature 'non-traditional' students are at greater risk because:

> *'(they) bring into higher education a much larger and more complex baggage of commitments and external constraints than 18-year-old colleagues. And when these are combined with the psychological demands of academic study they produce, for some, intolerable stress which tutors, counsellors and advisers try to relieve' (Wagner, 1990: 49).*

Sometimes these outside pressures are used as predictors of non-completion. For example, a representative of an Open College Network outlined the characteristics perceived to mark out students at risk of not staying the course:

> *'We used to have the following criteria of sustainability: academic credentials, accommodation, finance, childcare, health*

and support of partner. If a student was presented with problems in five of these areas, their chances of survival were virtually zilch. If they had three to five, we'd go for it but they would still need forms of support.'

However, it is often observed that while outside pressures of work and family prove too great for some mature students, many others manage to overcome similar pressures. Lucas and Ward (1985), for example, noted that many mature students at Lancaster University were able to overcome severe non-academic problems and achieved good results:

'thereby emphasising the determination of older students to make the most of a valued opportunity. A high level of motivation seems therefore to distinguish many mature students from normal age entrants.'

Motivation

A similar point has been made by Metcalf (1993): 'One factor, in addition to age, distinguishes mature students as a group: motivation.'

As seen in Chapter 5, several studies have found that mature students are currently slightly more likely than younger ones to complete courses. It has been suggested that this may be because students who remain in full-time education mainly because of the erosion of job prospects for school leavers are unlikely to be totally committed to study (Payne and Storan, 1995), whereas adults with work experience and those who have made considerable sacrifices in order to participate in further or higher education will be far more highly motivated:

'End of course perceptions of students reinforce the view that maturity, motivation and prior work experience are essential characteristics for survival on accelerated routes' (Foong et al., 1994).

Munn, MacDonald and Lowden (1992) found that adults taking mathematics, science and engineering courses were both highly motivated and strongly determined to succeed:

'The adults who went on to take these courses were likely to be those who had found solutions to, or at least thought they could deal with, problems arising from personal circumstances.'

Some further and higher education staff claim the image of adult learners as students needing 'remedial' support is far from accurate. The head of a guidance service at a new university reported that although she had expected to be mainly supporting mature students, it was the younger ones who needed most help: 'mature students are very much more "together"'. Similarly, Bargh *et al.* (1994) have observed that most mature students are skilled at time management and better able to organise their academic, work, social and family commitments than students of a younger age.

Bourner and Hamed (1987b) concluded that adults who complete part-time courses while holding down full-time jobs demonstrate skills that contribute to degree success: 'These capabilities might include the ability to organise time effectively, to study effectively, high motivation or simple tenacity.'

Integration into the Learning Environment

The possession of outside commitments, therefore, is not *per se* a predictor of non-completion. A more reliable measure would be the degree of support students, especially those who differ from the majority of the student body by virtue of age, race, disability or qualification received when they enter an institution.

Drawing on sociological models, Tinto (1975) argued that a student's ability to integrate into a learning environment has a major influence on whether they complete a programme of study. He identified one of the major reasons for not continuing as lack of integration, both socially and academically, into the life of an institution. The research evidence as a whole confirms that continuation on a course is positively associated with the degree of student involvement in institutional life. This has particular relevance for adult students, many of whom are part-time and choose to learn near their place of residence. Several studies (Webb *et al.*, 1994; Roberts and Higgins, 1992) have found that a large proportion of mature students study at institutions within relatively easy distance of their homes. Tinto noted that although non-residential students face less of an initial dislocation as they do not move away from their existing social and family networks, they tend to form weaker ties with institutional life because of this. As a result, they become less involved with the learning community than those who undergo a break in their social relationships.

Many studies of mature students have confirmed this analysis. Cullen (1994) found that Access students who had left the course lacked a sense of belonging to the group and had not developed a real involvement with the institution where they were studying. Metcalf (1993) referred to the sense of isolation adults can experience if there are few other mature students, if they are not resident at or near an institution or if they have family commitments and are therefore cut off from the social life of an institution.

Any student of whatever age who feels isolated, lonely, and out of place and who does not develop a sense of 'belonging' to the learning community is at risk of leaving a course in the early stages.

Treating Stated Reasons for Leaving Courses with Caution

There is a danger that the prevalence of non-academic factors among the stated reasons for mature student withdrawal might lead to complacency on the part of institutions:

> *'The notion that most drop-out occurs for non-course reasons is a useful rationalisation which could be used by adult educators to justify administrative inaction' (Hamblin, 1990).*

Hand, Gambles and Cooper (1994) argue that since the most significant reasons for the non-completion of adult learners are changes in personal circumstances specific to the individual, there are few preventive policy measures open to providers apart from provision of low cost courses and childcare facilities.

It is true that some students experience personal problems of such a magnitude that an institution is powerless to intervene. For example, Roderick, Bell and Hamilton (1982) found that the domestic and financial problems of some unqualified students at the University of Sheffield were so great that there was little the institution could do to help them.

Other researchers, however, have found that the causes of non-completion that are intrinsic and extrinsic to an institution are often inter-related and cannot be easily disentangled. Mansell and Parkin (1990) found that even where practical and domestic reasons played a part in non-continuation, dissatisfaction with classroom experience was frequently also involved. As Smith (1979) and others have argued, external and domestic pressures will more readily lead to a student abandoning the course if she or he is unhappy with it, whereas satisfied students with similar outside pressures will strive to continue. Thus many analysts warn against the facile conclusion that since the causes of withdrawal appear to be external to an institution, there is nothing the institution can do to prevent or ameliorate them.

There is, therefore, a widespread view that the stated reasons for withdrawal should be treated with extreme caution. As researchers in this field invariably point out, non-completion is a complex process which usually involves a combination of interacting reasons, of which only one or the most recent might be mentioned. Woodley *et al.* (1987) have given the clearest exposition of this process:

> '*If we are to arrive at a more complete understanding of why an individual drops out it seems that we must move beyond the usual "checklist" approach. We must take into account what participation means to an individual and the total context in which he or she is studying. We must treat dropping out as a complex process in that it generally involves numerous interconnected causal factors and often builds up over time. Finally, we must have a greater awareness of how people explain their behaviour, both to themselves and to other people.*
>
> *Each student will have a different array of factors which is relevant to his or her situation, and each factor will be weighted in importance by the individual. Drop-out will occur when, in some sense, the sum of negative factors outweighs the sum of positive ones. Some students will begin their course with the positive barely outweighing the negative, and these "marginal" students will be particularly vulnerable. Any small, new negative factor such as a cold classroom or missing one class may tip the balance. In other cases the positive factors greatly exceed the negative ones and it will take a dramatic new negative factor such as a death in the family or being sent abroad to cause withdrawal.*
>
> *When students are asked why they dropped out they frequently give the most important or most recent negative factor as a reason. In many cases this is a valid and sufficient response. However, many of the reasons, while valid in themselves, do not provide a complete explanation. For example, although moving house, changing jobs, pregnancy, etc. may be given as reasons for dropping out there will also be students who underwent similar experiences but still persisted with their course. To understand these different outcomes one needs a deeper awareness of the various positive and negative factors operating within a given individual, and the weight which that individual assigns to them' (Woodley et al., 1987: 162–163).*

Woodley *et al.* also argue that other variables come into play which make it unwise to predict completion or non-completion on the grounds of personal factors:

> '*A course with a highly educated, highly committed group of students may nevertheless have a high drop-out rate if it has a poor teacher. Similarly a course which is pedagogically excellent may have a high drop-out rate if it attracts large numbers of "marginal" students ... While a single factor may predominate, in*

general the drop-out rate will arise out of a complex interplay of course-related and student-related factors' (Woodley et al., 1987: 164).

Many researchers have subsequently confirmed the accuracy of these observations.

It has also been found in follow-up studies that students cite reasons for leaving courses which do not threaten their self-esteem or which they perceive as 'acceptable': 'Often the reason given at the time was either the last straw or the least threatening reason to reveal' (Cullen, 1994). As Hamblin (1990) observes: 'A student who drops out of a class may feel in their own estimation that they have failed and could be very sensitive about the reasons.'

Kember (1995) observes that lack of success is easier to accept if students attribute it to something outside their own control, such as competing work, family and social pressures. Thus a number of researchers have found that the stated reasons for withdrawing from courses sometimes act as proxies for others:

'One student explained her non-completion initially in terms of not having any teaching practice but in the interview it emerged that she had considerable feelings of inadequacy, lack of confidence and not being able to cope' (Harvey, 1995b: 179).

The stated reasons for non-completion can also be influenced by the way in which follow-up studies are conducted. Research findings indicate that respondents to postal questionnaires tend to give personal factors as the main reasons while those who are interviewed are more likely to cite institutional or course deficiencies (Hamblin, 1990). Mansell and Parkin (1990) also warn that tutors who are asked for information on the reasons for student withdrawal tend to bias their reports towards reasons which are external to the institution.

Woodley *et al.* (1987) have summarised some of the reasons why student responses to follow-up surveys should not be taken wholly at face value:

'First, the response rates for drop-out questionnaires are generally low. This leaves great scope for response bias, particularly if those students who are experiencing academic difficulties are less willing to give their reasons for withdrawal.

Secondly, ... it seems likely that students who find the courses too difficult or who fail to put much effort into them will seek to protect their self-esteem by attributing their withdrawal to external pressure such as lack of time.

Thirdly, even a "genuine" response of lack of time conceals as much as it reveals. In the sense that it means that students

> *prefer to spend their time on other activities it clearly relates to the perceived value and interest of the course itself.*
>
> *Fourthly, when main reasons are 'unpacked', features of the courses themselves are often revealed as contributory factors ... Changes in goals or intentions may also arise from the course itself: "I decided not to become an accountant because I realised from the course that I couldn't cope with the maths."*
>
> *Fifthly, certain factors can be attributed to the institution or to the students themselves. For instance, if students cannot cope with the level of the course they may blame either themselves or their teachers. It seem likely that mature students returning to education with some trepidation would adopt the former position' (Woodley et al., 1987: 162–163).*

The difficulty of identifying the real reasons for non-completion can cause a real headache for providers. This was demonstrated in the Cullen (1994) study, where it was found that the support offered to non-completing students was inappropriate in some cases because the underlying problems were not expressed:

> *'The impossibility of complying with an imminent essay deadline was used by at least four people as the opportunity to indicate a wish to leave and was met with offers of flexibility which would have helped if work pressure was the problem, but since this was only a "cover" this support was not effective' (Cullen, 1994: 10).*

This raises the question of what institutions can do to prevent student withdrawals if students do not divulge the true reasons for leaving. Fortunately, there are a number of common findings on the factors associated with non-completion which should indicate where intervention is possible.

Factors Associated with Early Non-Completion

A finding that is consistent across sectors and institutions is that the first term, semester or year of study is crucial. Most institutional surveys and research reports have found that withdrawal rates are highest among all student cohorts early in a programme of study and that the chances of successful completion rise significantly as students progress through a course (Davies and Yates, 1987). The following are typical responses from higher education institutions to the survey conducted for this project:

> *'Non-completion was highest during the first year of attendance. Fifteen per cent withdrew from first-year courses; 11 per cent*

failed or had to repeat and 5 per cent passed but did not re-enrol. In total almost one-third of our students falter on their first year.'

'Most students withdrew early on in the year with 63 per cent leaving during the first term and 72 per cent during the first semester.'

'The vast majority withdraw in the first year, with the third month the peak month for leaving for both full-time and part-time students.'

The factors associated with early withdrawal are well established. They include:

- inappropriate or rushed course choice
- lack of preparedness for level of work
- lack of background knowledge/grounding in a subject
- workload and time commitment greater than anticipated
- lack of academic skills such as essay-writing, note-taking
- frustrated expectations (of course/institution)
- difficulties in settling in and integrating into the life of an institution
- lack of support from 'significant others'
- lack of financial support.

Factors Associated with Later Withdrawal

- changes in personal circumstances:

    'The drop-out rate is highest in Autumn, followed by the Spring term. This suggests that if students are unhappy with a class they either drop out in the Autumn term or do not return for the Spring term, and if they drop out after that it is probably mainly due to changing personal circumstances' (Hamblin, 1990: 38)

- work-related factors: getting a job is a frequent cause of withdrawal among mature students, and those already in employment, particularly part-time students, often experience severe conflicting pressures
- achievement of desired goals
- financial problems
- domestic commitments or problems
- long duration of programme of study (Mansell and Parkin, 1990 refer to the difficulties of maintaining motivation when working for a distant end-qualification)

- apprehension at returning to study after losing continuity
- fear of or unpreparedness for examinations.

Many of these factors can be tackled by providers, as is outlined in Part 3.

Part 3
Strategies for Improving Retention

Chapter 8

Pre-Course Contact and Transition

The magnitude of student loss in the early stages of a course highlights the importance of good pre-course contact, information and advice, as well as the need for support and encouragement to students during the period of transition.

As the last chapters have argued, although many mature students leave courses for reasons that are ostensibly unrelated to the institution or course, these are often underlain by academic problems and dissatisfaction with their learning experience. The failure by many institutions in the different sectors to predict and address student problems is highlighted by certain points that recur in the institutional and research evidence, namely, the number of mature students who:

- receive little or no advice before starting an advanced course
- find course content and workloads far more demanding than they anticipated
- fail to notify institutions that they are leaving or do not give the real reasons for leaving.

Given that most withdrawals take place during the early stages of a learning programme, intervention at this stage is crucial. Mansell and Parkin (1990) claim that the extent of early withdrawal can be favourably affected by concentrating on the cycle of student support from pre-enrolment advice through to induction.

The Further Education Unit (1994) has recommended that to reduce wastage, colleges need to put efforts into the preliminary period and:

- provide accurate pre-course information
- ensure welcoming, uncomplicated enrolment procedures
- identify student-centred (work, domestic, study-related) reasons which might make sustained study difficult
- ensure that staff are available to provide specialist information, wherever possible, from those who will teach the students
- relate the relevance and appropriateness of the course to the students previous learning attainment and experience.

Pre-Entry Information and Advice

Webb *et al.* (1994) found that Access and alternative entry students frequently gain their education in an unplanned and 'haphazard' manner and often enter higher education without any formal guidance. Booth, Layer and Moore (1994) found that nearly 30 per cent of mature students had not sought advice from any source before entering higher education and had relied on prospectuses. Surveys of full- and part-time students at Chelsea and Kensington College indicated that very few had received any advice before entering a course. Other research reports suggest that a disturbing number of students enter programmes with insufficient knowledge of and preparation for what it will entail:

> *'One of the main reasons given (for leaving in the first term) was the students' lack of understanding of the degree of commitment/motivation necessary to complete a course of study' (Beddow, 1994).*

There is now a widespread consensus on the value of providing good pre-entry information and guidance. As Kember (1995: 208) observes:

> *'Students with little or no experience of education beyond school can have little insight into the expectations and conventions of academe.'*

Thus many reports have recommended that providers supply prospective students with more detailed and accurate information on course demands as well as independent guidance:

> *'Marketing and recruitment measures should provide individuals with a real insight into the nature of the programme and its progression routes, and ensure that contact is maintained through to enrolment' (Smith and Bailey, 1993).*

Some analysts suggest that better retention rates can be achieved through measures such as closer relationships between receiving and 'feeder' institutions and better pre-entry information and guidance. An HMI report (1991) referred to one college which had reduced its non-completion rate to 4 per cent by securing good communication with feeder schools, ensuring that students were well-informed and prepared, and developing appropriate starts to courses.

Other reports, however, refer to poor and fragmented links between institutions and guidance providers, although 'the increasing complexity and flexibility of education provision makes such clear, co-ordinated structures between providers and agencies imperative rather than just desirable' (Booth, Layer and Moore, 1994).

Munn, MacDonald and Lowden (1992) stress that though it is the quality of pre-entry advice rather than the form it takes that matters, face-to-face contact with a skilled and experienced tutor can significantly help to prepare students for the nature and demands of a learning programme:

> *'The need for a good match between student and course seems self-evident and yet it is by no means easy for either college or student to achieve. The complexity of factors affecting learning, the difficulty in specifying precisely what students need to know before embarking on a course, to say nothing about the institutional climate which students enter all make matching students and courses a difficult business. Opportunity to discuss a student's motivation, previous knowledge and personal circumstances seems especially important for adult students, who may be making considerable personal and financial sacrifices in returning to study. Such face-to-face consultation with a skilled tutor allows more thorough exploration of options than even the best produced brochure or prospectus' (Munn, MacDonald and Lowden, 1992: 9).*

There is, however, an obvious tension between the need for institutions to attract target student numbers and the need to provide potential students with accurate information and impartial guidance. The current situation in both further and higher education militates against the provision of impartial guidance, as has been noted in several reports:

> *'Institutions are under pressure to recruit as many fee-paying students as possible. Understandably they try to make their courses sound as attractive as possible, and it is tempting to underplay the amount of time involved or the prior levels of skill and knowledge that are required. Educational institutions should not be forced to behave like used-car salesmen. Rather they should be in business to guide people down the road' (Woodley et al., 1987: 167).*

> *'Marketing an institution and its programmes is not the same thing as providing information for potential users. While considerable strides have been made in the marketing of higher education institutions it is debatable whether the quality of information presented to applicants in order to assist them in making an appropriate choice has received equal attention' (Moore, 1995: 19).*

> *'Institutions seem to have difficulty in distinguishing their strategies for educational information and guidance from their*

strategies for student recruitment. The latter appear much better developed than the former. Increased competition for students had improved marketing and recruitment strategies, but this is not widely reflected in better quality student educational guidance' (Robertson, 1994: 13).

Thus although colleges are required by the FEFC to offer independent initial guidance, developments in further education combined with competition for students and the need to meet funding targets can conflict with this objective:

'Franchised courses, foundation courses and generally closer links between further and higher education can all have beneficial implications for access but can also restrict students' options by channelling them in specific directions.

The incorporation of further education colleges, along with the emergence of an increasingly competitive climate and the pressure to increase student numbers in line with government policy may lead to the temptation to guide potential students towards the most appropriate of courses on offer at an institution rather than towards ... other options. The temptation for guidance providers to hang onto a client rather than refer them to the most appropriate service undermines impartiality and works against collaboration between providers of guidance' (Booth, Layer and Moore, 1994: 152).

Informal reports from people consulted for this project confirm that some further education staff are afraid of losing students if they refer them on. Where judgments on employment contracts are made with reference to enrolment and completion numbers this is understandable.

The evidence suggests that there are also problems with providing guidance for evening class students and those who enrol by post. A number of research reports have commented on the fact that provision of guidance tends not to be available to students attending evening provision (Munn, MacDonald and Lowden, 1992; NIACE, 1995) although anecdotal evidence suggests that some are now asked to sign a document saying that they have received guidance in order to provide evidence for funding purposes. An FE informant reported that part-time students who had enrolled in person had had 'some conversation' with staff, but those who had enrolled by post had received no guidance.

What should be included in pre-entry guidance?

Research into early withdrawal indicates that prospective students need, as a priority, to be given explicit details on the timetable and the expected workload. From observations during their research, Munn, MacDonald and Lowden (1992) have identified the areas which they feel should also be included in pre-entry guidance:

- the subjects to be covered – with a comprehensive description of each along with information on the depth of coverage
- an exploration of the suitability of the course in relation to an applicants background experience and goals
- the entry qualifications or previous experience needed and an idea of whom the course is intended for
- a discussion of the workload (teaching hours, practical, home-study) and how it would fit in with the applicant's other commitments
- the type and frequency of assessments
- lists of recommended reading (pre-course and course texts)
- a staff contact name and phone number in case applicants want further information
- term dates
- costs
- career counselling (subsequent employment and educational options)
- information about alternatives (subject, level, mode) for those for whom the course is not suitable
- the opportunity to talk to or contact current/past students.

The Munn, MacDonald and Lowden study suggests that non-completion might be reduced if students entering advanced level courses in areas such as science and engineering were warned that they require some recent background knowledge and facility with mathematics. They therefore recommend that staff should try to assess the level of the applicant's background knowledge and its applicability to the course:

> *'Students felt disadvantaged by a lack of background know-ledge because courses were sometimes pitched at a level which assumed some prior knowledge. This had not been expected by those without this background experience and they felt over-whelmed when material was introduced which was at too high a level. Higher Physics staff told us that some previous know-ledge had to be assumed. Students realised too late that they should have been advised of this. This highlights the impor-tance of pre-entry advice.*
>
> *Our data also suggested that the length of time since that knowledge had been acquired was important. In general, we*

*found the more recent the knowledge the better. First, it meant
that concepts and ideas were fresh in students minds and they
did not have to spend time familiarising themselves with them.
Second, recent study of the area had allowed students to become
familiar with any changes in terminology or curriculum which
had taken place. And third, the adults were familiar with the
way in which these types of courses were taught and, thus, did
not have to spend time acclimatising themselves to being a
student' (Munn, MacDonald and Lowden, 1992: 12–13).*

Other areas that have been suggested for inclusion in pre-
course guidance are assessment of prior learning and experience,
diagnosis of possible problem areas and counselling about the
factors that increase the risk of non-completion.

Preparation for the experience of being a student

Prospective students need more than just information about the
courses they are intending to follow. Research reports frequently
stress the importance of providing information and advice which
honestly conveys the experience of being a student.

Many follow-up studies have found that students who discon-
tinued their programmes of study had experienced a clash between
their expectations and their actual experience of academic life. This
was particularly the case for those who had prepared for entry to
higher education in a more supportive, student-centred learning
environment. This highlights the need for what Kember (1995),
drawing on Tinto's (1975) model, calls 'normative congruence' –
the degree of fit between students' and institutions' expectations of
each other:

*'Normative congruence is achieved when a student's intellectual
beliefs and values are consistent with the expectations of the college and its faculty. In an academic context, incongruence is
most often present when a student's conceptions of knowledge
and student requirements differ from academic norms and conventions ... Integration will not occur if a student is unaware of
an academic convention or has a different perception of a task,
or an alternative conception of knowledge to faculty' (Kember,
1995: 49–50, 194).*

The physical environment can also be different from students'
expectations. It has been found that the size and anonymity of
formal institutions can take students of all ages by surprise.
Interviews with former Access students who had left university
courses indicated that they 'had not anticipated some of the broader
aspects of the higher education student experience' – not only

teaching, assessment methods, support structures and finance but also the size of institutions, classes and the student body (Booth, Layer and Moore, 1994). Case studies in a newspaper article reveal the disappointment of new students who had experienced classes attended by 80 people, lectures attended by 400, and tutors who did not learn students' names (Pritchard, 1995).

A study of students who transferred from the Open University to other higher education institutions revealed that 'the change from a highly structured, regulated, well supported mode of study to a looser more autonomous one' often 'generated alienation in a way that distance did not because they expected much more than the campus could deliver' (Rickwood, 1993: 31–32).

An honest picture of student life should be conveyed by promotional material. Closer links between institutions are another way of preparing students. This can involve visits from higher education staff and current students to colleges and adult education centres, and visits from students in colleges and other learning environments to higher education institutions. Several universities in Yorkshire run special workshops, and in one case a two-day residential course, to prepare Access students for university life. One uses a questionnaire on students' knowledge and expectations of higher education as the starting point for workshop activity (Appendix 3).

Some institutions have a trial period at the beginning of a course of study. The Open University has a provisional three-month registration period in the first year of study, at the end of which students can decide whether to pay the full registration fee.

The University of Sussex has a Welcome Weekend at the beginning of the year for students of all ages, their parents, family and friends, to introduce them to campus life and its facilities.

The Transition Period

The first weeks in a new environment can be difficult and disorienting, especially for those who have not done any formal learning since leaving school and those whose experience of post-school learning has been somewhat different from advanced study in a formal institution. Many individuals consequently feel isolated.

Utley (1994b) quotes a lecturer on the importance of helping students through this period and giving them a sense of 'belonging':

> *'Transition to life as a student whether 18 or 81 involves some complex emotional and psychological processes that are ill-researched and ill-understood. If students feel emotionally "held" by the contact with their institution they will proceed with learning in the same spirit of trust as a baby has. But if the*

> *student is made to feel small and dependent, some form of withdrawal from the institution may take place.'*

As Tinto (1975) has argued, a degree of social and academic integration is necessary if students are to settle satisfactorily into the life of an institution. This highlights the importance of inter-student and staff–student interaction. With distance study this can be difficult to achieve. According to a report by Payne and Storan (1995), group admissions have been used in some places to ease the transition to undergraduate level study for some groups of distance learning students. They refer to practice at the Open University, where students who have studied together on a lower level course elsewhere are sometimes encouraged to enrol on the same Foundation course.

Mentor schemes

Mentor schemes have been introduced in some institutions to help students through the transition period (Moore, 1995). HMI (1993: 6) refer to one institution where second-year students were paid to run a weekly session to help and encourage first-year students:

> *'Monitoring of the scheme showed a reduction in drop-out rates during the year and an improvement in end of year performance.'*

Peer support groups

The formation of peer support groups has also been advocated as an aid to students during the transition period. Metcalf's literature search (1993) showed that mature student societies and the establishment of support groups for those who are in a minority in an institution can assist integration by providing opportunities to socialise and discuss common concerns. Kember (1995) argues that support groups and group learning activities particularly help open and distance learners who have limited opportunities for student interaction, and part-time students who tend to form weaker ties with an institution than full-time students. However, he warns that:

> *'Merely issuing a list of other students' addresses, as commonly happens, seems to achieve very little. Self-study groups are more likely to be successful if the course design incorporates activities suitable for group interaction' (Kember, 1995: 192).*

Induction

Bourner and Barlow (1991) contend that good induction strategies that are designed to help students get more value out of their experience of education will be reflected in lower absenteeism and drop-out levels as well as better course work and examination results. According to the Further Education Unit (1994), induction procedures should include:

- discussion with students of the amount of work required outside the classroom or formal provision
- ensuring that students are aware of facilities (social areas, library, refectory, advice and counselling) and that part-time and full-time students enjoy the same facilities
- introducing students to course members and all staff teaching the course
- helping students to acquire study skills and to plan work.

As part of induction, some institutions also provide short introductory or orientation courses to help students adapt to the challenges of study.

A number of reports (e.g. FEDA, 1995) have concluded that induction needs to be a continuing process rather than a single activity at the beginning of a student's experience.

The institutional environment

The appearance, facilities and ambience of an institution are important in helping students to settle in. In some studies of student leavers (e.g. LJMU, 1995b), it has been found that the standard of facilities, particularly library, computing, study and social facilities, contributed to decisions to withdraw.

The Further Education Unit (1994) advises college staff to:

- ensure that the welcome area creates a positive, friendly image, with trained receptionists
- ensure classrooms and facilities are well signposted
- ensure refreshments and social areas are congenial, addressing both younger student and adult requirements.

Student reception

Kember (1995) argues that student progress is assisted both by the extent to which employers, family and friends support their learning and by the initial support and encouragement they receive in an institution. The attitudes and behaviour of teaching and administrative staff can have a strongly positive or negative impact on the morale of new students.

'I believe that all members of a college who have any direct or indirect contact with students will play a part in developing ... collective affiliation towards the institution. Warmth, interest

and perceived competence will contribute towards a sense of belonging. Coolness, tardiness in responding, bureaucratic indifference and incompetence will all have a negative impact which is often not perceived by those responsible for engendering it' (Kember, 1995: 203–204).'

The importance of staff attitudes, understanding and support will be explored in Chapter 9.

Chapter 9

On-Course Support

The progress and well-being of mature and 'non-traditional' groups of students often largely depend on the amount of support and understanding they receive in an institution. Good staff–student relations and the provision of practical and personal support for learners are the keys to better retention rates.

Institutional intervention should not be totally concentrated on the initial learning stage. As Metcalf has pointed out:

> *'Experience and difficulties will change over the course. Students may be seen as going through three stages: settling in, settled and preparing to leave. Few studies have identified needs at specific stages and their methodology limits their ability to do so. These changes need to be taken into account in the development of policy and it may be relevant to focus change on specific periods' (Metcalf 1993: 24).*

Similarly, Kember argues that providers need to recognise that student experiences change as a programme proceeds:

> *'Motivation will vary, often being strengthened towards the end as completion comes into view. Intrinsic interest will differ from module to module. The degree of both academic and social integration will be influenced by changes in student characteristics, development of goal commitment, the nature of courses, support from the institution and events and attitudes in the work, family and social environments' (Kember, 1995: 123).*

Thus students require continuing help and support throughout their learning programmes. A key aspect of this is the help and support of sympathetic staff.

Understanding Adult Learners

Metcalf has called for greater understanding of non-traditional learners if 'wastage' is to be eliminated:

> *'The evidence suggests a complex pattern of personal, institutional and external factors contributing to the performance of*

mature students which greater knowledge of the experience of mature students would help to elucidate' (Metcalf, 1993: 16).

Although further and higher education now have large numbers of mature students, there is evidence that staff attitudes and institutional practices have not entirely caught up with the needs of this clientele. The research literature suggests that while there has been action to encourage applications from 'non-traditional' student groups, in some institutions the reception they receive is not always sympathetic and comparatively few measures have been introduced to assist them to cope with any problems they may experience. NIACE (1995) found wide variations between further education colleges in the extent to which they consider adult learner needs and a lack of mechanisms to enable adult students to express their views. In higher education, Webb *et al.* (1994) have found that mature students, particularly those over 25 years of age, are likely to be perceived as 'non-standard, whatever their qualifications and previous educational experience. Some of the attitudes they experience are illustrated by the list of quotations from higher education students and staff on pages 142 and 143.

The research literature highlights the importance of recognising in programme content and delivery and teaching styles the previous experience, commitments and concerns of adult students. The literature suggests that mature student experience is generally ignored (Edwards, 1993) and rarely incorporated into curricula and course work. Staff also need to recognise in their attitudes and practices the psychological 'baggage' many adults carry with them when they return to education:

'Often adults return to education with a legacy from school of failure and of lack of opportunity, and a legacy from society about their age or class or about being female. These things are not taken sufficient account of and, unless they are, adults will continue to leave courses because the negative side of the balance tips too far down' (Cullen, 1994: 13).

Secondly, institutions need to take account of mature students' outside commitments and pressures. In their national survey of full-time mature students studying for a first degree or equivalent, Redpath and Robus (1989) found that 58 per cent of students aged 26-plus were married or cohabiting; 51 per cent were supporting children and 14 per cent were single parents (virtually all women): 'This suggests that a significant proportion of mature students have substantial family and financial responsibilities'. Thus it has been found (Wakeford, 1994) that many students view their learning achievements not only in terms of academic performance but also in terms of their ability to maintain a balance between their education and their work, family and social lives. Nonetheless the pressure of their outside commitments may only be noticed if it affects their academic performance. In her study of non-traditional students, Metcalf (1993) found that higher education staff often assumed all students could spend long periods on the campus; course deadlines and assignment requirements were not flexible and some staff failed to turn up to take classes or to keep appointments which mature students had made great efforts to attend. Students in such cases understandably resented the implication that their time was not valuable.

Although adult and community education staff and those teaching Access courses are generally sensitive to the needs of adults, the failure of educational institutions to recognise their other roles and commitments, and especially the pressures on women, is well documented. Cullen (1994) speaks for many other commentators when she asks providers to:

'acknowledge openly that many of their female students have to face the problem of finding affordable quality care for their children while they study. This does not necessarily mean providing such care: women are used to arranging childcare, to coping with finding alternative arrangements at the last minute. What it does mean is course providers changing their internalised image of what a student is like so that female adult students are made to feel acceptable as they are. The pressure of juggling the roles of student, partner, mother, worker, would be lessened if the role of student was seen as including, not excluding, the others' (Cullen, 1994: 8).

Thirdly, there is a need for institutions to recognise the specific difficulties faced by specific groups who lack recent educational experience or who find themselves in a minority in an institution because of their age, race, class, gender or disability:

'The ease with which students cope with adaptation to college social and intellectual life depends on how closely their academic conception and social circle match those of the college they are entering. The greater the difference between the norms of college behaviour and that of the student's home community, the more difficult the transition process will be. The obvious implication of this statement is that the greatest difficulties are likely to be faced by those from minority groups, overseas students, mature entrants or those from small rural or isolated communities' (Kember, 1995: 41).

The evidence suggests that non-traditional students in large institutions which provide little opportunity for interaction with members of staff and where staff display little understanding of their needs, are more at risk of non-completion than other learners.

Staff–Student Interaction

All the evidence indicates that good staff–student interaction is one of the keys to good retention rates. An Access Validating Agency which sent evidence for this project quoted one institution as finding 'noticeably higher retention rates on programmes with a low student–tutor ratio'. The expansion of student numbers, however, particularly in higher education, has made this more difficult. A study at a new university has found that about a third of former students claimed to have had good relations with less than 50 per cent of the staff with whom they came into contact (LJMU, 1995b). Yet most research into non-completion stresses the crucial importance of staff–student relations and informants to this project frequently referred to the vital role played by staff in student well-being. Many have found that it is often informal contact and rapport with a staff member – not necessarily a counsellor or a personal tutor or even someone with a formal pastoral role – that gives students the encouragement to continue studying. The key attributes of such a person are friendliness, availability and interest in the student.

Cullen (1994) found that students wanted staff to listen to them, respect their views and experience and acknowledge their concerns:

> *'They wanted to be listened to and the perceived gravity of their problems acknowledged. This approach is more respectful and probably more effective than trying to buoy the students through by downplaying their anxieties ... The ideal Access tutor was interested in every student, treated the students as a mature equal with valuable life experience upon which further learning was built, and enabled the students to engage in self-directed learning' (Cullen, 1994: 23, 19624).*

According to Munn, MacDonald and Lowden (1992), effective support from tutors involves:

- tutors being approachable and helpful
- the development of staff–student rapport being an explicit part of course design
- tutors treating mature students as equals
- tutors displaying a genuine interest in the students
- making available well-designed materials for those courses on which tutor contact is limited.

Munn, MacDonald and Lowden identified the following simple but effective measures for encouraging good staff–student relationships:

- students were encouraged to arrive early for classes so that they could chat informally with tutors and discuss problems
- classes were allowed to run on late so that students could ask questions or could work through areas for which there had not been time during the lesson
- staff and students took coffee breaks together
- tutors gave students their departmental (and sometimes home) phone numbers to encourage them to call if they were experiencing difficulties
- if students missed lectures, staff sent out lecture notes to them.

'All of these served to make the students feel valued and signalled that staff had a personal interest in students' well-being' (Munn, MacDonald and Lowden, 1992: 20).

Munn, MacDonald and Lowden found that the highest percentage of withdrawals was on the open learning mathematics modules, which they attributed to the absence of face-to-face contact with tutors and other students. The researchers suggest that tutors could support students on open learning and distance courses by ensuring that there is some face-to-face contact, taking a more proactive approach to contacting students, and ensuring that course materials are appropriate.

Helping and advising students

In common with other researchers, Cullen (1994) found that a significant proportion of students had left a course without informing staff. In some cases this had been because they had missed part of the programme and felt too guilty, embarrassed or worried to contact staff. Similarly, the research into retention rates at Sheffield Hallam University revealed that many students had not informed staff of their decisions to leave. The study indicated a need for closer and more regular contact with staff and greater clarity about whom to approach (for advice) and how and when to approach them (Moore, 1995).

An article in *Netword News* (undated) argues that it would help students at risk if all faculty and administrative staff who come into contact with students were prepared to go beyond a narrow interpretation of their role: 'even a few friendly words can mean that students will be prepared to contact a person if at some later date they need advice'.

It is a commonplace that students, particularly mature and part-time learners, look to teaching staff for advice. As a former further education staff member wrote in response to this enquiry:

> *'The reality of formal part-time study is that individual tutors can make or break a learner's experience. The tutor is central to the creation of the essential, supportive social environment of the classroom which reduces drop-out. We can talk till the cows come home about the vital importance of guidance but we are seriously in error if we do not acknowledge the pivotal guidance role of the tutor for the part-timer. For many the teacher is the guidance system.'*

Research studies (Moore, 1995; Munn, MacDonald and Lowden, 1992) indicate that staff are more prepared to discuss academic issues with students than personal or social problems and the evidence suggests that many staff receive no formal training in providing this kind of support. Nevertheless, Kember (1995) proposes that all who have contact with students should see their role as encompassing some element of counselling and he suggests that staff development workshops might help those who find it difficult to adopt a more pastoral role:

> *'Attitude change is often a difficult process but in this instance the process can be aided by a workshop which aims to make staff more aware of the apprehensions of new students and the problems they face. Students themselves could be invited to talk to groups of staff. Staff might then discuss ways in which they can help alleviate these concerns' (Kember, 1995: 204–205).*

Similarly, Munn, MacDonald and Lowden (1992) call for staff development to assist staff in responding to mature student information and advice needs:

> *'It is important that tutors have access to the kind of information that adults are likely to need or are able to refer them on to specific agencies or individuals who can help. Staff development which raised awareness of mature students needs and advised tutors on how to deal with adults problems would seem helpful.'*

Some colleges have found that a telephone helpline is effective in helping students with any problems they may experience. This can be particularly useful for students who have limited time to spend in an institution or who have restricted access to staff. FEDA (1995) cites a college which provides subject-specific telephone helplines, commenting that such a service provides a confidential and non-threatening individual support mechanism that is not possible within a formal class meeting context.

Designated staff members: Smithers and Griffin (1986) suggest that each higher education faculty should designate a tutor to have particular responsibility for mature students.

Encouragement of group cohesion: Many reports have emphasised the importance of making learning a satisfactory social experience and creating a sense of group cohesion among students, especially those taking part-time courses, whose ties with the course and institution may be frail. Students who feel part of a supportive group are more likely to continue on a programme of study than those who do not. Research consistently reveals that the opportunity to learn alongside like-minded people and to share experience and ideas is a strong motivating factor. This appears to be particularly the case with mature students.

Wakeford's survey of nearly 400 Access students highlighted the extent to which they valued the mutually supportive group culture which had emerged on the course and which they tried to maintain in higher education:

> *'Many interviewees believed that they would not have completed the Access course without the support networks which were built up between themselves and other Access students. Typically, they felt at home on the Access course because they fitted in, belonged to a group, had the same problems, and shared information' (Wakeford, 1994: 251).*

Capizzi (1994) has encountered Access tutors who resist the modularisation of their programmes precisely because they consider the supportive ethos of the learning group central to the purpose and success of Access. A corollary of this is that some individuals may experience problems if such a group is dispersed. Thus it is important, where possible, to try and maintain student support structures:

> *'The transition from first term to second involved choosing subjects and therefore being in new tutorial groups. It was clear that the benefits from friendships and mutual support built up in the first term were not being utilised in the second term because of this change in course structure. A time-tabled means of maintaining first term tutorial groups would reduce non-completion of the course by improving group identity and mutual support' (Cullen, 1994).*

Mansell and Parkin (1990) have also found that courses with an inbuilt group cohesion relating to the norms and values of a profession or calling, such as nursing or pre-care courses, often exhibit much lower rates of withdrawal than others. There can be a tension between the creation or maintenance of a co-operative group learning culture and the increasing emphasis on individual achievement and unitisation in post-compulsory education. To improve retention rates, however, it is vital for institutions to encourage group learning and group support networks, particularly in higher education, where expansion has led to larger class sizes and a reduction in student support.

Separate facilities: Some institutions have found that mature students appreciate the provision of separate classes or facilities. Examples include a department at Sheffield University which has introduced separate tutorial groups for standard and mature students and Oaklands College, which provides separate leisure facilities for adult learners. Some colleges also provide a special base room for students on Access courses, which proves:

> *'an extremely important psychological support to students, as well as a practical necessity for mature students with often a quantity of baggage that needs safe storage' (Mansell and Parkin, 1990).*

Help with finance: An increase in financial problems among students has been reported in all sectors. Many learners have been affected by reduction in local authority grants and exclusion from welfare benefits. Mature students are particularly affected by the reduction in the number of discretionary awards and the abolition of the Mature Student Allowance except for all those enrolled on specific progression courses before 1 September 1995. Redpath and Robus (1989) found that most mature student households had higher outgoings than incomings.

Those most affected by financial problems include: older students who have given up jobs to study, unemployed adults, single parents and others with homes and families to support, part-time students, students with non-working partners. According to Munn, MacDonald and Lowden (1992), the kind of financial problems these groups face are:

- difficulties in meeting mortgage payments
- trying to support a family on a low income
- delays in receiving grant or bursary payments and having to borrow money until the payments come through
- grants and bursaries being assessed at too low a level, with the result that students spent weeks, and sometimes months, trying to get these changed
- problems with payments from the Department of Social Security, particularly falling into the 'benefit trap', whereby the income support for the family would be reduced by the equivalent of any grant received.

Access funds (now frozen for three years) do not meet the scale of demand even at their current level. According to the CVCP (1995), about 30 per cent of applications are turned down. Those receiving Access Funds in 1993/94 included:

- self-supporting students without maintenance awards – 5 per cent
- students with dependents to support – 10 per cent
- students not receiving the full parental contribution – 10 per cent
- students living in rented accommodation – 65 per cent
- others – 15 per cent.

This suggests that the bulk of funds are going to younger students living away from home.

The Wirral Metropolitan College report on financial barriers (1993) found that even fairly small amounts of money for assessment, equipment, books or travel costs can affect the retention of unemployed students and others with very low incomes. Childcare is another costly item that many parents cannot afford. The report recommended the following strategies to help students facing financial hardship:

- better targeting of the Access Fund
- childcare expenses to be included in Access Fund criteria (e.g. small sums to pay someone to collect children from school)
- broader concessionary fee levels at the college creche
- an expansion of the College Hardship Fund
- provision of financial advice (the college has since appointed a student finance officer to offer advice to students).

Other institutions are also taking steps to help students with financial problems. Bradford College now incorporates financial advice in initial interviews. Some higher education institutions run job clubs or employment bureaux for students. According to the CVCP (1995), most universities also operate their own private hardship scheme, independent of the Access Fund, and some operate separate loan schemes.

Support for Particular Student Cohorts

Ethnic minority groups

Metcalf (1993) recommends staff development strategies to help staff respond better to the needs of ethnic minority groups, quoting a report for the Council for Racial Equality (Williams, Cocking and Davies, 1989) which identified problems such as a non-supportive environment, a lack of understanding of black student needs, racial bias in course content and lack of institutional action in response to racist incidents. She recommends development sessions to help staff examine course content and confront their own prejudices and suggests that practical support for ethnic minority groups might include: increased consultation with students and community groups; the appointment of a special student adviser and the establishment of mentor schemes and centrally co-ordinated support groups.

Students with disabilities

Metcalf (1993) also calls for staff development to raise awareness of the needs of learners with disabilities, a group that remains generally under-represented and neglected in the post-compulsory system as a whole. A survey by the Labour Party (1990) found that between 33 per cent and 38 per cent of higher education institutions employed staff with specific responsibility for the welfare of disabled students. In 60 per cent of the responding institutions, about half of facilities such as lecture theatres, classrooms, residential and dining halls were wheelchair-accessible; 76 per cent provided special residential accommodation but only 17 per cent provided transport services. For deaf students, 64 per cent of polytechnics and 44 per cent of universities provided sound systems in lecture halls. Some provided other aids such as tactile maps, large-print VDUs and special library rooms.

Metcalf's literature search revealed that students with disabilities face particular difficulties in relation to dependence on tapes; examinations and assessment approaches; the organisation of classes and delivery; speed of speech; discriminatory language and behaviour; and lack of consultation about the kind of facilities and premises required.

Metcalf quotes research claiming that only about 25 per cent of staff teaching disabled students had received special training. She recommends the list of support measures for groups with disabilities, drawn up by former polytechnics in collaboration with Skill, the National Bureau for Students with Disabilities (Polytechnic of North London, 1991):

- a written equal opportunities policy that is separate from a general equal opportunities policy
- a named person for staff and students to turn to for advice
- policy and practical guidelines for examination procedures, which should be known to staff
- support for students on courses from teachers, counselling and advice staff, careers staff

- practical support such as help with computers and study skills support
- good physical access arrangements and sign-posting of sites and buildings
- staff development, including awareness training for staff
- advice and help with finance.

Carers

One of the biggest problems adult learners experience is a conflict between their role as carers and their role as students. Although, as Cullen (1994) suggests, it would be unrealistic to expect every education provider to offer inexpensive and high quality childcare without resources being made available for this purpose, they should, nevertheless, put pressure on those who control budgets to make childcare facilities, allowances and advice more widely available for those who require it.

In further education there is growing recognition of the pressures on carers. FEDA (1995) cites some colleges which have extended childcare into the evenings and weekends and cater for children aged over the age of eight. Another report refers to colleges which were seeking European Union funding to help adults providing for elderly and sick relatives to undertake education and training (*Guardian*, 12 November 1994).

Higher education students studying in further education colleges

It has sometimes been found that groups of mature students flourish better in the more intimate learning environment provided by colleges than in larger, more anonymous higher education institutions. As a result, some commentators have expressed support for the idea of adults studying entire higher education programmes within a college environment:

> '*Franchised courses can frequently provide a much more appropriate learning experience than that given within higher education institutions. They provide a unique academic halfway-house in an often familiar environment ... classes tend to be much smaller than in HEIs, staff are more accessible, the quality of pastoral care is greater and students have the support of like-motivated peers. Feedback from adult students who have progressed to higher level study at the franchiser institution suggests a far lower level of satisfaction' (Bird, Crawley and Sheibani, 1993).*

Brady and Metcalf (1994) report that mature students often choose to take franchised courses because of a college's proximity to their place of residence. They identify other advantages as greater teacher–student contact and smaller groups. To compensate for the disadvantages associated with such courses referred to in Chapter 6 (fewer facilities than in higher education; students' sense of isolation from other higher education students), they recommend the following support measures for higher education students studying in further education colleges:

- staff development both prior to and during the franchise arrangement, not only to build up subject matter expertise but also to prepare staff for the required managerial role
- strategies to encourage students to feel that they belong to the main institution as well as to their local college (regular visits would help)
- opportunities for higher education students in colleges to meet other higher education students and provision of social facilities to support such interaction
- provision of enhanced library facilities with improved supply of books and journals and study space.

Part-time students

A number of reports have called for the enhancement of guidance and support for part-time students, many of whom, especially if studying away from main sites or attending courses in the evenings, have access to fewer services and facilities than full-time students (NIACE, 1995; LJMU, 1995b).

Unemployed students

Dekker and Whitfield (1989) found that two-thirds of unemployed students with transport problems withdrew from college courses. They suggested that the college might organise some form of transport for students in its own interests, as well as theirs. In some rural areas (e.g. Hereford) colleges are collaborating in the provision of free bus services for students who would otherwise have no means of getting to classes.

Some of the Problems Encountered by Mature Students in Higher Education

Quotations from students

'I asked if I could change my tutorial group as all the people in my group were young lads straight from school and were so much more confident than me. I was told that they behaved that

*way because they were all very bright students headed for
"double firsts" so of course I couldn't compete with them.'*

*'I had one of my tutorials on Friday. As I live in another town
(and have a family to look after) I wanted to have that day free
from travel. But they said they couldn't fit me into another
group – and besides, it would create a precedent.'*

*'They said I was welcome here, but they haven't changed any-
thing to make me feel as if they meant it.'*

*'I wanted to get some recognition for the degree course I didn't
complete, but they told me I couldn't and that I'd be better off
trying to start again at another institution which didn't know
anything about my previous uncompleted course.'*

*'They said they could arrange for me to get my wheelchair in
for the entrance exam. They made arrangements for me to use
an entrance around the back and the goods lift. The only toilet
I could use was in the basement and it hadn't been cleaned for
a long time.'*

*'I said I was on an Access course. He (the Admissions Tutor)
told me to go and do A-levels in maths and English.*

*'They told me how hard it would be – with being a lone
parent and so forth – but they didn't tell me how they would
help me.'*

*'I didn't know that there was a Mature Students Society. Nobody
told me.'*

*'The Union is just for kids – so are all the bars and lounges. I feel
so silly in there.'*

*'I didn't expect to be treated as though I were still at school.
I suppose it's because of the way the younger students behave.'*

Quotations from staff

'Taking Access students means taking worse students.'

*'Why don't we just tell them to get A-levels – it's their fault for
not having them.'*

*'Mature students take up more time than they are worth –
they've got so many problems and it's not my job to deal with
them.'*

*'Mature students are OK but they always need study skills,
don't they?'*

'Of course we've got an Equal Opportunities Policy – but what has not having a crèche got to do with that?'

'If we don't get black students that's their fault – they don't apply.'

'Why should we change our curriculum, our subject content and our so-called institutional culture for students from ethnic minorities? Our overseas students manage very well without special provision, don't they?'

'We'd like to get young ladies on our Science and Engineering courses but although we've done everything to get them here they don't want to come because they don't like these subjects, do they?'

(Source: YHAFHE, 1993)

Chapter 10

Academic Support

Many students, especially those with little recent learning experience, require assistance in returning to formal study, and all aspects of a learning programme should be designed to offer them maximum encouragement and support. All students should be offered guidance and some may need additional elements of support such as preparatory courses or some refurbishment of study skills.

Many mature students have experienced an interval since they last undertook some form of study and some re-enter the education system with a legacy of failure dating from schooldays. Their progress and what Kember (1995) calls 'academic integration' depend heavily on the nature, extent and quality of the academic support they receive:

> *'Some form of academic support for those who feel out of their depth in the first term because of their lack of previous education would enable more students, in particular those from traditionally non-participant groups, to complete the course' (Cullen, 1994).*

> *'Unqualified students need special attention. What is clear from this study is that if students are left to sink or swim, many will sink' (Roderick and Bell, 1981).*

Woodley *et al.* (1987) recommend that learning support strategies take account of the following:

- previous level of academic achievement
- student preparedness for the workload/commitment
- student satisfaction
- personal and professional difficulties which can disrupt study, including changes in employment situation
- students readiness for study and subsequent technical competence at studying
- student perceptions of progress
- the appropriateness of classroom experience for the individual, including pace of learning, nature of learning experience and relationship with tutor

- timing of courses and required attendance patterns
- the degree to which the institution gives persistent messages of value and support.

All aspects of the learning experience should provide academic support, including:

- the curriculum
- course design and delivery
- teaching/learning methods
- tutor support
- guidance
- assessment support
- supplementary or remedial support
- study skills
- student self-help activities
- recognition of achievements
- access to libraries, computer services, etc.
- supplies of books, materials and equipment.

Curriculum and Course Design

It has frequently been observed that adults like to relate the subject they are studying to their existing knowledge, interests and experience. However, some have commented on the apparent remoteness of the further and higher education curriculum from the lives and concerns of many students. Weil (1986) has questioned the ability of higher education to provide non-traditional learners with an education that is relevant to the learning agendas they bring. She compares this with non-formal learning which often builds on learners' personal and employment experience. Williams, Cocking and Davies (1989) have also questioned why the higher education curriculum has been subjected to so little scrutiny:

> *'Courses in Humanities and Social Sciences ostensibly value personal experiences but frequently fail to recognise and validate knowledge, culture and experience from black communities. Other subject areas may not even make rhetorical claims of interest or question their ethnocentricity.'*

McNair (1993) argues for approaches to learning which stress relevance to personal experience and motives and help individuals to integrate their learning with their personal conceptual frameworks. Lack of connection with a subject can dampen a student's interest.

Other commentators have called for curriculum design to take greater account of the ways in which adults learn. Mason (1989), for example, argues that providers should be sensitive to the newer models of adult learning:

> '*This may involve designing non-standard courses for non-standard entrants; courses which require a radical reassessment of taken-for-granted assumptions about subject areas and which are open-ended and involve a degree of flexibility of choice hitherto unknown.*'

Course design also needs to take account of the nature and motivations of the student body. Kember (1995) suggests that students who are 'intrinsically motivated', i.e. interested in learning a subject for its own sake, are more likely to be 'academically integrated' than those who are extrinsically motivated (e.g. studying for a qualification), but their interest can be diminished by courses which are mainly devised to 'test their ability to reproduce bodies of knowledge presented by the faculty' (Kember, 1995: 195).

Harvey (1995b), however, has observed that students studying for external reasons such as to gain a qualification are often more highly motivated than those studying out of interest or for self-development. Lee (1991) has also found that course design needs to respond to the tendency of many adult students entering higher education to expect tangible results from their learning experience:

> '*For those of us working in the arena of higher education, teaching methods and pedagogic philosophy were based upon the experiences of delivering courses to the typical A-level entrant. Our mature students shared a very different set of expectations, which most academics are not very well rehearsed in addressing ... a pragmatic "common sense" ideology of education born of the harsh realities of the modern workplace and which undoubtedly owed much of its character to a decade and more of "free-market" rhetoric. This led students to regard the course that we were offering primarily in terms of a commercial exchange and fostered in some students the expectation that unless they came away from each evenings study with a quantifiable number of communication skills or a set of "facts" about communication which could be applied directly and immediately to their daily lives, then somehow they were not getting full value for their investment.*'

Teaching and Learning Methods

As we have seen in Chapter 5, mature students tend to perform far better in the social sciences and humanities than in the physical and natural sciences. Mason (1989) questions whether difficulties in learning scientific concepts should be attributed to the ageing process and a decline in mental processes, and suggests that they may be more connected with the curriculum, teaching methods and assessment. He argues that an important question we are failing to address is whether adults approach or understand scientific concepts in a different way from younger learners.

There is some agreement that teaching staff need to adapt their instruction methods to adult students. As staff in one higher education institution have found:

> *'We had to rethink our teaching methods and modes of assessment. Listening to and taking notes from a 50-minute lecture, essay-writing techniques, academic research, and making presentations to an audience were all skills which the average A-level entrant has begun to develop by the time he or she reaches higher education. For a middle-aged car worker or a 20-year-old secretary who has left school with minimal qualifications such activities must appear completely foreign' (Lee, 1991).*

Flexible and Individualised Learning

Mansell and Parkin (1990) recommend that rather than attempting 'to improve or ameliorate a group experience that is unsatisfactory to a proportion of its members', tutors should employ an approach which recognises the individuality of personal learning styles, pace and expectations and bases the learning experience on individual support and counselling:

> *'In our experience, real breakthrough comes with the introduction of flexible learning methods, with their built-in guidance, counselling and student-centredness.'*

The Further Education Unit (1994) has incorporated Mansell and Parkin's recommendations in its list of strategies to help further education colleges improve retention rates. This includes:

- monitoring students' perception of their classroom
- experiences and ongoing support
- checking that the pace of teaching and learning is appropriate for individual learners
- providing students with course objectives, activities and work schedules in advance
- identifying preferred learning methods where alternatives may be appropriate (e.g. more structured lessons or more informal groupwork)
- organising time for students to discuss their work, and ensuring that part-time students also receive tutorial support

- providing learning enhancement through workshop activities.

Many studies emphasise the need to design learning in such a way as to ensure early success and boost confidence (Pupynin and Crowder, 1995). According to Munn, MacDonald and Lowden (1992) learners' confidence can also be raised by pacing come content so that there is a gradual increase in difficulty, and by using feedback from students to inform/change course design:

'Such methods derive from the premise that although every adult is unique, starts from a different base and works at a different pace, they all share the common need to have their confidence in their ability to cope reinforced. By easing adults into course content, encouraging early success and thus building confidence, it was thought possible to overcome the disadvantage of no previous subject background or of several years away from study.'

Pupynin and Crowder suggest that students are likely to withdraw if a course turns out to be significantly different from their expectations. This could be avoided by regular review of expectations and goals.

Weil (1986) and McNair (1993) advocate the involvement of learners in the negotiation, control and management of their own learning. This encourages people to become independent learners and take responsibility for their own progress, a development which, according to Kember, contributes considerably towards successful completion, particularly by adult learners and distance learners with outside commitments and constraints:

'Successful students are those who internalize responsibility for their own progress. They negotiate with their families, work colleagues and friends to establish a time slot for study. The process is almost inevitably accompanied by mutual sacrifices by both the student and the immediate family. Those unable or unwilling to make sacrifices and negotiate a study sanctuary tend towards the negative track and to attribute any unsuccessful outcomes to factors external to their control.

Those who continue to externalize responsibility or learning outcomes will not progress. Those who accept responsibility for their own progress are on the positive track to success' (Kember, 1995: 219 and 207).

All the evidence therefore underlines the need for training programmes which assist staff in developing student-centred learning approaches. The study for BTEC (Smith and Bailey, 1993) concluded that personal attention is the basic principle behind good retention rates: 'The over-riding objective in encouraging good retention rates is to emphasise the importance of developing systems which give as much individual attention as possible to our students'.

Provision of Basic Texts and Materials

Students need an adequate supply of basic texts and materials to support courses and access to the facilities and equipment necessary for independent study. This seems a very obvious requirement, but it is not always met. Clare (1995) cites inspection reports which refer to inadequate stocks of books and journals to support courses in some universities and acute pressure on library places in others.

Cullen (1994) refers to the efforts made by teaching staff on one Access course to improve library services for Access students by having a named contact person for students on the library staff and increasing the number of copies of basic text-books and photocopies of important articles.

Guidance

The argument for better educational guidance is frequently made. It is alleged that after the introduction of the guidance service pilot voucher scheme, Employment Training drop-out rates fell from 45 per cent in 1990 to 10 per cent in April 1992 (*TEC Guidance Update*, March 1993).

During their learning experience, mature students are likely to need information and advice on a wide range of issues:

- issues and problems related to the current programme studied
- qualifications and progression routes
- other education and training courses and application procedures
- the personal and learning support services provided by the institution
- careers advice
- financial advice
- other sources of help and advice.

Munn, MacDonald and Lowden found the highest levels of satisfaction among students taking courses which were specifically designed for adults and which incorporated in-depth guidance:

> '*Access and the Open University students were much more likely to say that the guidance they had received had been in-depth, addressed their personal needs and was useful. This*

*is hardly surprising since guidance at all stages tended to be an
integral part of the design of these courses. Students on "main-
stream" courses were far more critical. Over half of the students in each of the two Central Institution case-studies were
unhappy with the guidance' (Munn, MacDonald and Lowden,
1992: 16–17).*

Although further education has recognised the importance of
guidance and many colleges now have special guidance units and
specialist staff, higher education seems to lagging behind despite
developments that underline the desirability of providing guidance.
As McNair (1993) has pointed out, while higher education has
become more diverse, complex and flexible, offering students more
opportunity and choice, it has also created more opportunity for
confusion, mistaken choices and wasted effort. However, reports
claim there is a lack of a strategic approach to guidance in most
higher education institutions (Roberston, 1994). This is borne out
by several institutional reports. Although some universities have
special guidance and student support units, others, as Booth, Layer
and Moore (1994) have found, have no clear routes or central referral points for guidance, which results in adult enquirers being
'passed around' from person to person.

Guidance needs to be available to all students – whether full-
time, part-time or open learning, at all times of the year and at all
stages of the course. However, many reports indicate that it is not
available for part-time and evening class students or that, when
available, it is under-used by such students, who do not see it as
being genuinely open to them.

Many studies also stress the role of the tutor in the guidance
process. Munn, MacDonald and Lowden (1992) typically found
that mature students had made little use of college-wide guidance
provision other than the careers advisory service and that most had
sought help from their tutors. As indicated in the previous chapter,
some staff development is required to help them fulfil this role.

Forms of Supplementary or Remedial Help

Preparatory or introductory courses

For those undertaking advanced courses in areas which require
recent background knowledge, some preparatory classes may be
necessary. Munn, MacDonald and Lowden (1992) have found that
in subjects such as the sciences, engineering and technical subjects,
familiarity with the subject matter is a distinct advantage and that
to progress satisfactorily, students need a general foundation on

which to build and a grounding in basic concepts. They set out the advantages and disadvantages as follows:

Advantages	Disadvantages
Foundation on which to build	Courses may be pitched at a level which assumes some existing knowledge
Familiarity with subject concepts	Difficulties in dealing with scientific and mathematical concepts (e.g. how to conceptualise maths)
Familiarity with scientific/ mathematical ways of thinking and so able to deal with quantitative arguments	

Workshops

The Further Education Unit (1987) found that the two areas that present most difficulty to those without recent study experience were the ability to write discursive prose and the ability to work with mathematical concepts. From their work in five further education colleges, Mansell and Parkin (1990) suggest that retention can be improved by additions to the 'normal classroom diet'. They found the most effective of these were workshops which enabled students to sort out academic problems in a different environment, using different materials and according to their own pace of learning. The kinds of help offered include:

- drop-in workshops in areas such as maths, English, assessment of prior learning and experience, portfolio-building
- foundation courses to increase background knowledge
- self-help teaching packages
- drop-in careers advice with help in areas such as form-filling, CV preparation, interview practice
- courses on study skills.

Study Skills

Adults who have been away from education for some time often require help with getting back into the way of studying. Munn, MacDonald and Lowden (1992) point out that being able to study effectively is not necessarily something which comes naturally: 'It may take students months to learn how to organise themselves and their work so that they are using their time efficiently and getting the most out of study'. However, their study revealed that teaching staff seemed to assume that mature students were already equipped with study skills or that they would pick them up 'in a sort of osmosis fashion'. The skills that emerged as important in this study were:

- time management and self-discipline
- note-taking:
  - to ensure that information was in a summarised form for later revision
  - to help students clarify their ideas
- continued practice with problem-solving exercises:
  - to understand the methods and concepts
  - to develop a facility in problem-solving
  - to find out why they were making errors
- report- and essay-writing:
  - to present results and information concisely
  - to develop expertise in written presentations
- using the library.

Many of the students in the Munn, MacDonald and Lowden study felt that they had received little help with the development of such skills. There is some evidence, however, of an increasing awareness of its value. A number of further and higher education institutions now provide separate classes or drop-in workshops on study skills and some provide self-learning packages.

The Centre for Research on Learning and Instruction at the University of Edinburgh has developed an integrated computer-based package for staff and students designed to pick up weaknesses in individual students' study methods and strategies, to provide information to staff on students who may need specific forms of support and to provide advice to students on study skills and strategies.

Assessment Support

In his study of mature students in further and higher education, Roderick (1981) found that assessment methods posed major difficulties for many adult learners. Particular problems mentioned were difficulties with examination and essay-writing techniques, slowness in organising material and poor memory. Many were good at performing in seminars but these were not assessed. The majority of mature students in one study preferred continuous assessment, 'a proportion that increased substantially with age'.

Munn, MacDonald and Lowden (1992) also found that continuous assessment was favoured by adults because it provided them with regular feedback, revealed how well they were doing and indicated areas that needed improvement. It was also seen as less threatening than end-of-year examinations. Students taking a large number of different subjects or modules, however, had more mixed feelings about continuous assessment because of worries about the extra pressures that might be involved.

The evidence indicates that students appreciate the following:

- specific instructions on what is needed in an essay
- clear explanations of grading schemes
- rapid turn-round in grading and returning assessments
- practice in examination techniques and provision of model responses
- frequent and regular feedback on performance.

'The quality of comments and speed of return of assessments were very important. Students felt that there was a danger that, if it took a while to receive feedback, then they would have moved on to a different topic and have forgotten the previous one' (Munn, MacDonald and Lowden, 1992: 24)

Many make the point that feedback should be positive and include detailed comments and constructive criticism. Kember (1995: 117) perceptively describes academic study as:

'rather like a game with rules, conventions and codes of behaviour. To be successful, a student has to learn the rules and integrate behaviour with the accepted norms. Leaving school early has deprived the student of exposure to academic conventions ... Constant rebuttals in the form of low grades for work which the student thought was good would clearly lower the perceived benefits of continuing with the course.'

HMI (1993) refers to a practice that has proved effective in one higher education institution. This involves holding timetabled tutorial sessions to provide feedback on essays. Pairs of students are asked to read each other's essays and come with prepared comments.

Munn, MacDonald and Lowden (1992) suggest that a short handout containing guidelines for writing essays and examination answers and providing model answers would be relatively simple to produce and would help to give students an idea of the standard required.

Recognising Achievements

Many courses leading to vocational qualifications award credits for each completed unit. Those leading to academic qualifications, however, tend to award a single qualification on successful completion of a long period of study. There is increasing criticism of this 'all or nothing' approach to advanced qualifications which means that many people who have to leave a programme for reasons beyond their control gain no recognition in terms of credit for their learning and achievements up to that date: 'the implication is that time spent on a course has no value if a student drops out' (Temple, 1991).

The evidence suggests that many learners are motivated by the possibility of achieving short-term goals and credit which provides evidence of the progress they have made. Woodley (1992) noted that 'dormant' students with low qualifications who gained some course credit appeared to gain more benefit than their counterparts with higher qualifications.

It is argued that the greater availability of relatively small units of achievement would not only assist learners who need to study in an intermittent way but would also assist transfer across academic and vocational systems (McNair, 1993; Robertson, 1995). According to McNair a growing number of higher education institutions have adopted the CNAA Credit Accumulation and Transfer scheme but in most cases its full potential has not been exploited: learners often pursue credit-rated courses without much use of the added flexibility available.

Student Self-Help

In a study conducted for BTEC (Smith and Bailey, 1993), students said they valued peer group support and shared working. Mutually supportive groups can considerably assist adult learners who lack confidence in their academic ability and, especially, those who are involved in open and distance learning. The advantages have been described by Munn, MacDonald and Lowden:

> 'Adults often feel less inhibited about discussing their problems with their peers rather than with staff. Second, helping someone else with their work is a very good way of testing one's own grasp and understanding of the material. And third, students are able to contact each other as and when they come across problems rather than having to wait until their next class' (Munn, MacDonald and Lowden, 1992: 22).

In the Access courses covered by the Munn *et al.* study, staff had engendered group cohesion by encouraging students to help one another. However, attempts to encourage self-help groups among open learning students had been less successful, mainly because of students' doubts about the value of getting advice about mathematical problems over the telephone and diffidence about contacting people they had not met or hardly knew. This suggests that providers need to be more proactive in helping students set up their own self-help groups.

According to McNair (1993), some institutions are experimenting with structured peer tutoring within institutions. This involves students 'teaching' or supporting each other on an individual or group basis within a framework established by the institution.

Reactions to Academic Support

Mansell and Parkin (1990) warn that providers should not expect that all students will welcome improved support measures. They cite some instances of resentment and resistance when staff have attempted to provide better guidance and induction services and monitor student satisfaction. They found that part-time students with severe time pressures and limited class contact hours particularly resented any class time being devoted to learning support measures.

Similar reactions have been noted by people consulted for this project. For example, some further education staff have found that potential enrolees resist attempts to offer them pre-entry guidance. Likewise, Cullen (1994) reported that the majority of non-completers in her study either loved or hated study skills depending on whether they had other commitments. Munn, MacDonald and Lowden (1992) found that the value placed on study skills support was inversely related to whether or not it had been received: those who had received it tended not to value it highly, while those who had received no formal help with study skills were likely to say that they would have appreciated this kind of support.

Some studies suggest that students do not use support services because they are not sufficiently promoted or publicised. Student surveys at Kensington and Chelsea College (1995) revealed that while a majority of both full- and part-time students had not used academic support services, a significant proportion claimed that they did not know of their existence. In Cullen's (1994) study, some former Access students had perceived student support services as exceptional rather than as an integral part of the course, and some did not feel they had a right to use them.

Such evidence suggests, firstly, that academic services should be available and promoted to all students, including part-time and open learning students. As FEDA (1995: 21) suggests, however, different levels of support may be appropriate, depending on the student group and the programme:

'It may be appropriate for a distinction to be made between:
(a) provision of (an identified level of) support for all students

on certain programmes; (b) entitlement to (further) support for students on some programmes; (c) access to (a defined level of) support by individual students in any college programme to differentiate between anticipated levels of need or demand.

Critical points throughout the learning programme should be anticipated when the college may provide extra packages or careers planning and guidance sessions.'

Secondly, where possible, some forms of learning support could be integrated into programmes of study, not as a separate element taking time away from the content, but as an integral one. If learning support became a permanent feature of programmes, and access to additional academic support structures were promoted as every student's right, resistance to unfamiliar and unanticipated aspects of the learning experience might be reduced.

Chapter 11

Provision of Student Support Services

There are wide differences between sectors and institutions in the amount and quality of support they offer students. Expansion of higher education appears to have led to a diminution in the support provided and, particularly, in staff–student contact. The evidence indicates that effective student support measures require (a) a holistic approach and (b) managerial commitment and clear policies. Improved procedures for advising potential leavers are needed in both sectors.

Differences Between the Sectors

Individual institutions vary widely in the nature and quality of the student support services they provide. However, the evidence suggests that further education colleges are generally better at providing support than higher education institutions (Payne and Storan, 1995).

The difference between sectors was reflected to some extent in the responses to this enquiry. When asked what measures or strategies were in place to improve retention rates, staff responding on behalf of further education colleges cited a wide range of services and policies (figures in parentheses indicate number of responses):

- a policy on attendance monitoring/tracking (9)
- tutorial system/personal tutor support (5)
- financial support (5) (e.g. financial advice, free courses, payment of examination fees, financial help with travel and childcare, financial aid schemes, fee remission)
- improved pre-entry information and guidance for all students (4)
- improvement of general student support services (3) (e.g. appointment of a student support officer; establishment of central student support services; the establishment of counselling and welfare support services linked to admissions)
- improvement of academic/learning support (3)

- provision of on-course and drop-in guidance (3)
- modularisation of courses (2)
- improved induction procedures (1)
- 'customer care' training for staff (1)
- counselling services (1)
- an electronic register system (1)
- improvement of facilities for students taking higher education courses (1)
- the development of a comprehensive programme of community-based courses (1)
- better careers counselling (1)
- health education counselling (1)
- stricter entry qualifications (1)
- a student entitlement structure for both part-time and full-time students (1).

The higher education respondents were less forthcoming. Only three mentioned measures to increase retention rates, which were:

'Some pre-entry courses, maths for instance, introduced to retain less able students. Usual services such as counselling in place.'

'Student services and tutorial counselling.'

'Increased emphasis on academic and personal counselling.'

Responses from two old universities suggested some complacency in attitudes towards retention rates:

'In theory all aspects of our work should do this.'

'This (question) assumes that retention/withdrawal is a problem. There is a need to establish what is an acceptable loss rate. We have no proactive measures, more preventative ones such as personal support systems. Also, some factors leading to withdrawal are beyond the control of the institution.'

The Consequences of Expansion

There are, of course, many individual examples of good practice in universities. The Educational Development Services Unit in the Centre for Access and Advice at East London University co-ordinates learning support across the institution, including specialised provision such as assistance with English language, dyslexia, special needs and study skills (Payne and Storan, 1995). There are signs, however, that the combination of expansion of student numbers and static resources in higher education has led to a deterioration in student support services (Brown and Brimrose, 1992; HMI, 1993). In their report on student support services in former polytechnics and colleges of higher education, HMI (1993) comment on the negative consequences of expansion such as deterioration in the provision of initial information and induction services and unsympathetic staff attitudes:

> *'The poorest practice was seen in institutions experiencing the most rapid change; where policy appeared overnight and staff were not consulted; where students were taken on an "all comers" basis and the nature of support was for students to find a staff member who would listen to their difficulties. Student support services were frequently inadequately staffed, badly sited and poorly publicised. In these institutions, managers, staff and students all expressed dissatisfaction with the system.*
>
> *In some institutions, students in a degree foundation year for mature students and people with non-standard entry qualifications were given inadequate academic support and felt inhibited from expressing their learning difficulties because staff were unused to dealing with learning difficulties and the lack of confidence displayed by students' (HMI, 1993: 16–17).*

Other consequences of expansion have been overcrowding of classes and lectures and weakening of tutorial support systems (McNair, 1993). One report refers to increasing impersonalisation of teaching and learning processes, larger lecture and tutorial groups and loss of individual contact between students and teaching staff. As a result 'the holes in the net through which students can fall become larger' (Payne and Storan, 1995: 36).

A study of teaching standards in 100 higher education institutions found that in some departments, students were being poorly taught by overstretched staff in overcrowded lecture halls; contacts between students and lecturers had been reduced; small-group teaching was rapidly disappearing and classes of more than 200 were becoming commonplace. Some departments had a high failure rate in the first year:

> *'These are the consequences of the abrupt introduction since 1991 of mass higher education, accompanied by a 25 per cent cut in funding per student and strong incentives to institutions to boost recruitment' (Clare, 1995).*

Personal student support services have also been affected. Carlton (1994) has reported that students wanting counselling support could wait up to three weeks because services had reached bursting point:

> *'The enormous expansion in student numbers has not been reflected in the number of counsellors. Between 1989 and 1992, the ratio of students to counsellors doubled from 2,868 students per counsellor to 5,381 ... Counsellors have found that students are presenting them with more complex problems than before: financial problems and pressure to achieve. At the new universities, counsellors have found that the increase in Access students and mature students has affected the service, as they often face most difficulties. In 1992, mature students were 32 per cent of the total numbers of students who went to counsellors. A head of counselling at one university said "we cannot go out of our way to promote the service because we are already overwhelmed".'*

Recent studies confirm many of these findings. A survey of students who had transferred from the Open University to other higher education institutions revealed that they were experiencing far less help and support at their current institution than they had received at the Open University. Particular complaints concerned slow turn-round of course work, lack of feedback, minimal face-to-face contact with staff, poor staff time-keeping, difficulties with contacting staff, double booked or unsuitable accommodation and crowded or under-resourced libraries (Rickwood, 1993).

A study at a new university suggested that the personal tutor system had virtually collapsed but had not been replaced by any alternative support models:

> *'It was thought that higher education was becoming increasingly impersonal as student–staff ratios increase, and developments such as Cycle 1 are implemented. Greater flexibility of study and widening student choice correlate with the need for more student guidance as do higher numbers of non-traditional entrants. However, this ... sits very uneasily within the reality which many students saw of the low priority given to pastoral duties within university management' (Moore, 1995: 37 and 40).*

Lack of Support for Part-time Students

A disturbing finding from both sectors is the lack of support available to part-time students. In a project conducted with further education colleges, NIACE (1995) found that the extent to which on-course guidance, learning support, language support and study skills assistance was promoted to part-time students, especially those not based on main sites, varied considerably. It was observed that adult learners and their tutors were not considered a priority in terms of rooming allocation, particularly if they were part-time. A report on the reasons for non-completion at Liverpool John Moores University (1995b) stressed that part-time students should not have to compete with full-time ones for access to computing facilities, set texts and administrative staff time.

A useful resource to help institutions provide support for part-time learners has been produced by the Further Education Development Agency (FEDA, 1995).

Developing Student Support

It is clear that good student support services are urgently required if retention rates are to be improved, especially now that a significant proportion of students are moving to higher education from other learning environments where they have become accustomed to a higher level of support:

> *'The development of learning support strategies within higher education will not only ease the burden of increased student numbers without increased resources but make the progression of students to higher education much easier. Students who have become used to the level of study support in the best colleges not only need but expect ongoing support, not only for specific disabilities, but also to fill the gaps which come from having an interrupted education and to support students who are continuing to live at home in circumstances which are not conducive to study' (Payne and Storan, 1995: 37).*

The need for improved student support services has been recognised by some institutions, especially those which have initiated research on non-completion. The study at Sheffield Hallam University is a good example of how research into retention rates can generate or contribute to innovation. The strategies mentioned include:

- a student contact scheme: a mentor-type programme which matches small groups of Level 1 students with a Level 2/3 student who is taking the same programme. They meet two or three times a term. Free soft drinks are available during the meeting
- leaflets for students considering leaving or changing course and for staff involved in providing them with information and guidance
- a guidance service providing an additional central point to approach
- special training sessions for staff

- a training session for staff in the enquiry office during the Clearing period
- extended induction for new students, with information and guidance desks available
- enhanced student handbooks and course guides
- involvement by the Division of Access and Guidance in training course representatives (Moore, 1995: 43–44).

The university has also instituted Open Days especially for students coming through the Clearing process. This is designed to introduce them not only to the university but also to the city of Sheffield, since it has been found that many students arrive at the university with little knowledge of the geographical area they will be living in for the next few years.

Other institutions have also taken initiatives to increase retention rates. Smith and Bailey (1993) have described the measures taken by Stockport College of Further and Higher Education in response to concerns about non-completion among students taking an HNC course in Business and Finance. The course had a high proportion of mature women students and the main problems appeared to be volume of work, problems with the quantitative elements of the programme and lack of confidence. Strategies to improve retention included:

- recruitment, information and guidance designed to ensure that students understood the nature of the programme
- induction, including discussion of ways in which students might involve employers in supporting their study
- confidence-building incorporated into the early stages of the programme
- one-to-one tutorials timetabled to occur five times a year
- provision of learning support.

A 'key feature' of change was the conscious alteration of the culture of the programme. The programme team decided to be 'more nurturing and caring, and to advertise this to students to help them admit to having difficulties'. These measures allegedly reduced non-completion from about 15 per cent to 5 per cent.

A new 'Connections' scheme at Norwich City College ensures that non-traditional learners are supported both academically and personally throughout their progression through learning programmes. The initiative, which pays particular attention to details such as overcoming barriers, tutor and room allocation, has senior management support. Some consider this as the key to successful support and retention strategies:

'Making an attack on drop-out should be a matter of acknowledged college policy at all levels.

> *In the cases where student drop-out had been successfully reduced, the staff involved had received decisive support from senior management in the form of resources for the establishment of, for example, mathematics workshops, or in the form of a policy' (Mansell and Parkin, 1990: 15–16).*

Similarly, HMI (1993) found the best practice in higher education institutions with clear policies on student support:

> *'where the needs of specific groups are identified and linked to the provision on offer; where there is good communication between departments and services and a determination to ensure adequate provision ... where, although students may be experiencing personal difficulties, they know where to go for support and are pleased by the quality of support given. Staff are not isolated in their support work, which is well co-ordinated.'*

HMI (1993) put forward the following set of proposals for improving student support services:

- the co-ordination of management of support services
- a clear statement of entitlement for all students at the beginning of a course
- channels for voicing concerns
- targeting of specific groups for specific support
- quality control which takes account of non-academic aspects of institutional life
- the dissemination of good practice: 'the value-added elements of student support should be recognised'.

Staff Development

The enhancement of student support services has obvious implications for staff development. The areas in which tutors might need specific help have been listed by FEDA (1995) as:

- structuring of induction and group tutorials
- managing individual tutorials
- help with operating helplines (e.g. how to make supportive interventions)
- writing support materials (with attention to clarity, appropriateness of style and consistency)
- familiarity with student entitlements and referral routes.

Supporting Potential and Actual Leavers

Whatever the amount and nature of student support offered, there will always be some learners who want or are obliged to leave a programme of study. It is disturbing therefore that, according to the evidence, a significant proportion leave without discussing their decision with a member of staff. It is even more worrying that those who do inform staff are not always informed whether they are entitled to credit, advised about alternative courses and different modes of study or referred to internal guidance systems. In the Sheffield Hallam study, it was also found that staff were unlikely to discuss the more wide-ranging implications of leaving, such as entitlement to further mandatory awards. Such findings suggest that institutions need to establish more effective procedures to help staff assist students who are considering withdrawal:

> *'While there is a need to address personal concerns in a supportive manner, other more academic issues need to be addressed: the options of temporary withdrawal and part-time study, in addition to ensuring that people get credit for what they have done, may be particularly important if the problems are perceived to be temporary. Students may then be more likely to view their change of direction in a positive way'* *(Moore, 1995: 24).*

Strategies to assist students who are considering leaving would be largely the same in both the further and higher education sectors, as several research reports suggest. Essentially, students need to know who they can approach, and when, to discuss any problems they are experiencing, without fear of being pressurised into staying on a course. If students are encouraged to approach staff at an early stage, this can help to prevent minor problems turning into major ones (Moore, 1995). Thus the Further Education Unit (1994) has recommended that colleges:

- ensure students know from where and from whom they can receive advice and guidance
- ensure staff are able (and trained) to deal with more personal issues
- examine the role of tutor as counsellor
- identify and counsel students intending to drop-out
- follow-up absent students and maintain communication with them by telephone or letter.

A report from Liverpool John Moores University (1993) proposed that:

- written guidelines be provided for both staff and students on the consequences of and alternatives to withdrawal
- students be advised on the extent of existing flexibility, so that those who are considering changing or leaving courses can benefit

- efforts be made to maintain contact with temporarily withdrawn students to encourage them to maintain a relation with the institution and prepare them academically and socially to return
- help and advice be offered to students considering withdrawing.

One further education college which responded to this project now has a 'retention service' which supports staff in their pastoral role by contacting students at risk and encouraging them to continue their studies. Another claimed that retention has now become a key issue for all staff:

'All course teams are required to produce a retention strategy. A series of information bulletins has been published and issued to all staff. These stress the importance of regular attendance and of notifying college of absence or study problems.'

Contacting students who have ceased to attend

The evidence from some institutions is that it is not difficult to contact students so long as it is done shortly after they have left. However, this requires staff to notice, or to be promptly notified of, the student's absence. One report suggests that it is all too easy for some students to drift from temporary into permanent withdrawal without anyone noticing. For such students, especially if they are part-time, contacting an unknown student counsellor may not be an option:

'It is easy for part-time students to cease working on a course without informing anyone at all. When they find a course diffi-cult or do not make sufficient time available for study, they can simply decide to cease working on the course. It is all too easy to gradually drift into this situation by progressively falling behind schedule and eventually feel that they cannot meet assignment deadlines. While this process is happening, there is little incentive to contact a counsellor. It would seem to some to be an admission of failure. Others might perceive that there would be little that a counsellor could do to help. Whatever their perception of the value of counselling, there can be little incentive to contact a name in a telephone directory who might well be based at a distant campus' (Netword News, undated).

The article recommends that staff keep in touch with absent students, sending them classnotes for the sessions they have missed and reassuring them that they will not be isolated if they return to the class. Hamblin (1990) also suggests that the fear of returning to a class after a period of absence could be avoided by a telephone call or card from the tutor. Norton Radstock College contacts missing students by letter every three months, offering any support necessary, and circulates a newsletter, to both completers and non-completers, which includes success stories and encourages contact networks between ex-students (Harvey, 1995b).

Other (more expensive) 'catch-up' strategies might be telephone tutorials or the distribution of open learning materials to accompany the work conducted in class.

Although adult students are the focus of this report, the support strategies outlined above are applicable to all students and could improve retention rates among those of all ages.

Chapter 12

Conclusions

The project confirmed previous research in finding that:

1. there is a chronic lack of reliable data on the extent and nature of student withdrawals from post-compulsory education courses

2. neither funding systems nor institutional practices have fully adjusted to the fact that adult learners now compose a very significant proportion of the further and higher student population.

Data Deficiencies

There are significant discrepancies in the ways in which different institutions record student data such as qualifications on entry, student numbers, retention and non-completion rates. The problems many institutions are experiencing with keeping accurate student records noted in Chapter 3 suggest an urgent need for more central guidance and training, as well as for improved computerised systems and software.

To achieve an accurate picture of current patterns of completion and withdrawal would require institutions:

- to establish systems for data collection and recording that are both internally coherent (e.g. use of the same definitions of withdrawal across an institution), *and* compatible with the systems and definitions used in other institutions
- to present data in forms that make clear the distinctions between the different withdrawal routes taken by students and which recognise the distinctions between temporary and permanent withdrawal.

Greater convergence between the different sectors in their definitions of withdrawal and presentation of data would also contribute to a clearer picture. Although there has been some merging of the leaver codes used in the further and higher education sectors, the information available remains very disparate.

The evidence as a whole suggests that, although there are wide variations between institutions, non-completion rates in both further and higher education are increasing and are particularly high in some subject areas. However, *perceptions* of non-completion rates vary: some perceive them as unacceptable and others as reasonable. There is evidence, for example, of some complacency, especially in higher education, based on the belief that the reasons for withdrawal are often beyond the control of the institution. Follow-up studies indicate that this is not always the case and that dissatisfaction or unhappiness with the institution or course often combines with personal problems to bring about a decision to leave.

Use of Data

Current funding and quality control measures are encouraging institutions to monitor their retention and withdrawal rates more closely. However, such data should not be used merely to judge the efficiency of institutions or programmes. The Robbins Report (1963) referred to 'wastage rates' as the crudest criterion of the effectiveness of teaching in an institution and, over 30 years later, others are still making the same point:

> *'Levels of loss and withdrawal are, in themselves, poor measures of the quality of the learning system. A significant proportion of people in the system as it is currently structured and operates will not withdraw, irrespective of whether they are motivated to learn and/or getting anything from learning and/or satisfied with the experience ... It is also inevitable that a proportion of individuals will be lost due to changes in their own personal circumstances, irrespective of levels of motivation and the value they are getting from learning' (Hand, Gambles and Cooper, 1994: 33).*

> *'Some level of attrition is inevitable, however well the institution fine tunes its instruction and services' (Kember, 1995: 220).*

> *'Completion may be less an indication of institutional fitness than one of individual stamina and motivation' (Open University, West Midlands Region, 1995).*

It is clear that leaving a course of study should not invariably be seen as a sign of failure, either on the part of the individual or on the part of the institution. As argued in Chapter 2, withdrawal can be a positive step for many individuals: some gain employment and many, as suggested by Tight (1991), will have learnt something 'if only about themselves'. Many others move to other courses or other institutions. To quote again a comment from one of the individuals consulted for this project: 'What surprised me was that so many so-called drop-outs are actually back in. People aren't leaving education. They're shifting around.'

It is a fact of life that people's choices, aspirations and circumstances change. For many, leaving may be the right decision and the system should be able to accommodate this. This does not mean that we should not be concerned about non-completion rates. However, we should be concerned for the right reasons: not just because non-completion results in an institution losing money (although this is a legitimate and understandable concern), but also because it indicates that some students do not acquire what they want or expect; that some are ill-advised (or, more probably, not advised) and consequently make the wrong choice of course or institution; and that some experience problems on-course that are potentially soluble given the right kind of intervention, guidance and support. We should also be concerned that people who leave after a substantial period of study often have no tangible evidence of, or credit for, the learning they have put in. Moreover, some incur unanticipated financial, social and personal penalties as a result of withdrawing.

These factors should be of paramount concern at a time when further and higher education systems are increasingly opening up to 'non-traditional' entrants, many of them mature students with few qualifications and limited recent experience of formal study, and many with a legacy of previous educational failure. However, the evidence collected for this investigation indicates that it is funding criteria that concentrate minds on retention rather than the quality of student experience. In most institutions, evaluative tracking systems are internally- or institutionally-focused rather than student-focused.

Thus concerns expressed several decades ago are equally if not more relevant today:

> *'If large numbers of students who enter an open door discover that it is in reality a "revolving" door and that all they are doing is entering it in order to be carried round and out again, then both the education institution and society could be held to have erred ... It is not just a case of making initial places available for all who want them which means that society has fulfilled its obligation towards equality of opportunity and whatever happens after that is not its affair' (McIntosh, 1975: 174).*

> *'Moves towards mass education will be of limited value if they result in high withdrawal of non-traditional entrants' (Benn, 1994).*

Completion data should, first and foremost, act as a benchmark against which an institution can attempt to improve its academic provision and student services in order to enhance the learning experience of the student:

> *'It may never be possible for every enrolled student to graduate but improvement should be possible. Student progress statistics can be used as an indicator of the effectiveness of improvement measures. The ideal would be to move towards a climate of continual monitoring and searching for improvements akin to a total quality management approach' (Kember, 1995: 220).*

The Role of External Factors in Non-Completion

It is clear, however, that some factors outside the control of institutions have contributed significantly towards non-completion rates. There is little doubt, for example, that the expansion of student numbers in higher education without an equivalent increase in resources has had a negative impact on class sizes and has reduced student support services and direct staff–student contact. This has inevitably played a part in non-completion in that sector.

Secondly, the inflexible way in which many post-compulsory qualifications are designed does not help adult learners, in spite of the fact that mature students now constitute the majority in many institutions. One informant to this project described qualification routes in further education as 'a morass', with the three main 'tracks' – A-level, GNVQ and NVQ – inflexible and definitionally incompatible:

> *'There is no common language to describe the different qualification achievements and values, so it is very difficult to transfer from one to another. It would be far better if we adopted the kinds of advice given on a national credit framework as suggested by FEU or followed the example of Wales, where there has been piloting of credit transcript summarising all credit gained in different places and set in a common currency.'*

Funding arrangements

Thirdly, as Part 1 of this report has sought to demonstrate, institutional funding criteria based on traditional learning arrangements and time-scales sit uneasily with the more flexible learning patterns developed over the last decade and favoured by many adults.

> *'Increasing flexibility within the system helps people have a life outside the learning environment but funding mechanisms are not in tune with this' (Uden, 1994).*

The linking of funding to student growth targets and completion rates does not assist institutions with large percentages of adult students whose outside commitments oblige them to learn on an intermittent basis. To quote again two respondents working in further education:

> *'There is an implicit conflict between the growth targets and the demands and realisation of ordinary people's lives, exacerbated by a narrow perception of outcomes which does not acknowledge the concept of interrupted learning so common among adult students. This flaw in the funding methodology works against part-time adult students, who are particularly likely to choose this mode to fit in with the other demands of their lives and whom we must cater for in increasing numbers to fulfil government targets' (Whittaker, 1994).*

> *'The notion of drop-out is particularly damaging to adults compared with other students. We need to demonstrate the concept of interrupted learning. We get unfairly penalised for people taking time off for living' (FE staff member reporting to this project).*

As argued by Alan Tuckett, Director of NIACE: 'the concepts of more and different (students) and the average unit of resource are incompatible.'

A number of other commentators have criticised the tendency for institutional and student funding models to be largely geared to full-time students following fixed, time-limited programmes despite evidence that flexible learning modes are gradually changing the structures of learning, and the difference between part-time and full-time modes is shrinking:

> *'A persistent but flexible commitment to learning does not lend itself to the carefully enclosed courses with which we are familiar. Although some 900,000 students in HE formally study full-time, this is largely an administrative convention. In practice, large numbers of "full-time" students are being forced effectively to study "part-time" in order to maintain jobs, families and so forth. The distinction by mode of attendance between "full-time" students and the 400,000 who are formally "part-time" is beginning to look increasingly arbitrary and obsolete. This has long been the case in FE and funding formulae have begun to reflect this' (Robertson, 1995: 275–276).*

> *'The concept of a course, assuming as it does a group of students with near identical needs, may have a limited future' (Stott, 1994).*

'A new system of funding higher education is needed to share the burden between part-time students who pay their own fees and full-timers who do not. With the move towards modular and credit-based learning systems, the division between full-time and part-time is breaking down and HE is becoming more flexible, particularly for those unable to do a traditional three-year degree' (Times Higher, 21 April 1995).

An important and growing aspect of this flexibility – transfers between institutions – is also hindered by funding methodology. McIntosh (1975) argued several decades ago for the further development of inter-institution transfers, particularly for mature students:

'Any genuine extension of open admission... will have to allow for people who need to move from one institution to another for a variety of reasons. It is no longer adequate for institutions to deal with this problem independently. It is a luxury that neither the country nor potential students can afford.'

There is little indication that this advice has been heeded. As outlined in Part 1 of this report, transfers are often treated as noncompletions for funding purposes and institutions can be financially penalised when they occur:

'There's a lot of shifting (between institutions) going on. This needs a collaborative attitude which isn't actually present because of the funding system. The problem is that funding only follows institutions' (Open University staff member).

As a result, institutions are not as prepared as they might be to facilitate outward transfers. Anecdotal reports suggest that the importance of student numbers and retention rates in current funding arrangements have led to concerns about safeguarding institutional or programme funding and, sometimes, individual jobs. This, counterproductively, leads some staff to try and 'hang on' to students or to enrol unsuitable ones rather than refer them on to more appropriate comes or institutions. Rickwood (1993) argues convincingly that if funding is too closely linked to completion, a tension develops between an individual's changing preferences and the institution's desire to minimise its outflow: 'Need the success of the one in moving to a more appropriate or beneficial course be construed as failure for the other in not retaining the student?' He quotes Clark Brundin, former Vice-Chancellor of Warwick University, on the desirability of facilitating appropriate transfers:

'Completion can only be assured if appropriate programmes are being pursued. Flexibility is also essential, so that once it is clear that the individual and the programme do not match,

transfer to another programme is possible. The transfer may involve a change of institution but that should not be recorded as non-completion. Some value is added at every stage of the education provision and we must find ways of measuring this.'

Rickwood (1993) found that the chances of gaining admission to other establishments depended on what individual admissions tutors knew and thought about credit transfers rather than on any institutional policy or guidelines. Yet, as Rickwood argues, institutions need to work together to enable freer movement between them and encourage student autonomy:

> *'The most effective response to the autonomous student is a joint one. This sees the choice offered as one which stretches across institutions, and completion is more loosely defined not only in terms of where it occurs but also the length of time it takes. This suggests three models of student transfer: a* baling out *model when a university fails to satisfy. The threat to revenue and reputation of excessive baling out suggests institutions may see transfer as an export/import equation, albeit one in which importing is a virtue and exporting a vice. The broader view suggests a value-added model in which all institutions benefit from a freer trade within the larger setting' (Rickwood, 1995: 12).*

Robertson (1995) has proposed that a credit-based system would more readily accommodate adult learning needs and patterns, and funding based on credit would be both more realistic and more equitable:

> *'One way of ensuring greater equity in funding arrangements while retaining flexibility is to exploit the potential of credit systems. Just as credit-based learning provides the means to dissolve distinctions between modes of attendance, qualifications and sites of learning, so credit-based funding has the capacity to act as a currency to meet the flexible needs of learners. Not only would resources follow learners in ways which learners could influence but institutional providers would have an interest in responding more directly to learner choices. Choice in this respect concerns not merely the initial decision of which institution to attend – a choice which is only notionally available to most adults anyway – but decisions concerning the character and purpose of the learning experience, the pace at which it is enjoyed, the ability to interrupt progress for whatever reason and the capacity to move between courses, qualifications and institutions. This is not a great deal to ask. Yet a funding regime which expects most students, in HE at least, to sign on for one course at one institution and stay there*

continuously for three years is not one which has equity, choice or flexibility in mind (Robertson, 1995: 275–276).

Taken as a whole, the research literature and information supplied for this project suggest that learning systems and funding methodologies are, to a certain extent, pulling in different directions: while the former are moving gradually and cautiously towards greater flexibility and innovation, the latter are tending to constrain flexibility and innovation through over-emphasis on the traditional full-time, conventional learning model. All the evidence implies that there is a need to design more flexible funding methods which do not penalise institutions or individuals when students are obliged to interrupt learning, take longer than expected to complete particular parts of a course or move to a more appropriate course, institution or learning mode.

Acknowledging the Centrality of Adults in the System

As has been argued in Part 3 of this report, the first step in improving retention rates would be for institutions to acknowledge and accommodate the experience and needs of a more diverse student body. However, as Lee points out:

'Improving access is not just a matter of opening the doors of our institutions a little bit wider. It is not enough to pack more students into lecture theatres or duplicate existing courses and their traditional methods of delivery.

Mature part-time and non-standard entrants come to us with needs and expectations which often differ radically from our "core" student body. This requires adequate resources, and not only in terms of administrative and technical support. We need to be able to provide that critically important time and space, both for those who teach and those who learn, in order to allow them to rethink and adapt their long-held assumptions about the function and nature of higher education' (Lee, 1991).

Although adult students are sought by many institutions in order to meet their growth targets, few have fully adjusted their procedures, course provision, teaching practices and support services – and the assumptions underlying them – to an adult clientele. Robertson (1995) has observed a 'cultural resistance' in universities towards adjusting their procedures to a more diverse student population. In some institutions admissions systems are still largely geared to the conventional school leaver cohort, and, as demonstrated in Chapter 10, mature applicants often receive conflicting messages from administrative staff and admissions officers about the entry qualifications they require.

McNair (1993) argues that a system dominated by adult students requires structures which enable recurrence, intermittent learning, part-time opportunities and portable accreditation:

> *'What is logical and perhaps the only rational route for a 19-year-old may not be relevant to a returner in her late 30s. It is easy for funding and management systems to neglect this and opportunities for accreditation and qualifications need to be designed to encourage rather than obstruct them.'*

Institutional Conservatism

However, as Tight (1991) points out, there is still a deep conservatism within higher education, where each deviation from dominant models of provision and practice:

> *'has to be carefully justified and is then effectively limited and controlled through the range of checks and balances that exist to maintain standards within the system. These constraints are essentially self-administered. The major driving force behind them is the desire of most polytechnics and colleges of higher education to be though of as comparable to the universities and of the universities to be thought of as comparable to Oxbridge or at least their image of it.*
>
> *Change within established institutions is OK so long as it is relatively small-scale and gradual in its impact. In the great majority of cases, therefore, deviations remain confined to particular aspects of provision or to certain courses only. From this perspective, the significant point about the Open University is not its practice of open access or its use of distance teaching, but its retention of the honours degree pattern and the three-hour unseen written examination. Similarly, Birkbeck focuses on part-time students but follows in curriculum, teaching and assessment methods the patterns and practices of full-time provision.'*

Thus the evidence also implies that despite widespread moves towards modularisation, many providers still are resistant to change. Commenting on the fact that many higher education institutions still follow the traditional academic year, Robertson (1995) observes that they are not yet ready to accommodate:

> *'the flexible learning careers that will be required in post-Fordist labour markets as individuals move in and out of formal*

education and training, varying their engagement by time, pace, place and sponsorship.'

Similarly, McNair (1993) argues that our perceptions of higher education have yet to catch up with the changes that have taken place in the system:

> *'We have been holding on to the traditional model of the three-year Honours degree as the benchmark of what higher education is, although the experience offered to a self-financing, part-time student in an institution with a staff–student ratio of 1:22 cannot be the same as that of the school leaver, studying full-time on a grant in residence at a university with a staff–student ratio of 1:8.'*

Robertson (1994) has noted that despite the volume of institutional commitment to modularisation and credit accumulation and transfer arrangements, many institutions have not yet developed these to their full potential. He observes that in some institutions, flexible arrangements are regarded as marginal options for very small groups of individuals:

> *'It is apparent that neither credit nor modularity are yet seen as essential elements in the institution's portfolio.*
>
> *It is not clear where there is simply limited demand for credit transfer or whether demand is suppressed by institutional, financial and cultural factors. Unless policies define inter-university credit transfer as a desirable object, and make it possible for students, it is unlikely to expand.'*

The diversity of educational routes taken by mature students nevertheless underlines the importance of a framework which allows credit accumulation and transfers.

The Debate about Standards

Open access policies which admit non-traditional applicants increase the risk of higher withdrawal rates. This has been repeatedly pointed out over a number of years:

> *'The clear implication of extending access is that it increases drop-out. In the past, the "formidable selection device" – A-levels – meant that the majority of people never have a chance to "drop in" ' (McIntosh, 1975: 173).*

> *'The price of a very liberal entry policy is likely to be high dropout in the first year but many regard this as worth paying' (Bourner* et al., *1991).*

The evidence indicates that many institutions have not yet fully recognised the implications, for students, of a more open and accessible post-compulsory system. As pointed out by McNair (1993), as the system becomes more open and flexible, so the opportunities for confusion and mistaken choices increase. The Higher Education Quality Council (1994) has stated that a mass system of higher education must be underpinned by comprehensive, effective and impartial guidance and learning support systems. Yet according to Robertson (1994) and other analysts, guidance does not yet receive sufficient strategic support and resourcing in many institutions. This is surprising given the view that is fast gaining currency that some institutions are accepting students who are neither ready nor equipped to undertake advanced courses. Several recent articles have claimed that institutions, particularly the new universities, are admitting too many students who are not up to the required intellectual standard: 'the evidence suggests that the unconsidered expansion of higher education has spun out of control' (Clare, 1995).

To a certain extent, institutions are being criticised for a situation that is not of their own making. Policies on expansion of student numbers linked to funding allocation have inevitably affected admissions policies and put pressure on departments and admissions officers to recruit the right *number* of students rather than the right *students*. Thus the imposition of target numbers militates against the provision of impartial pre-entry guidance. Since providers need to acquire units of resource they will understandably try and recruit the numbers of students required to obtain the maximum number of units. This has inevitably had a detrimental effect on marketing and admissions practices in some institutions:

> *'The "shortage" of students in science and engineering means that the distinction between old and new universities is overlaid by a distinction between those departments which "recruit" students and those which "select". In other words, is the department's main objective to fill the places available (and which from 1994 it will be penalised financially for not filling) or is it selecting from a large number of well-qualified applicants (and will be penalised financially for over-shooting on its target)?*
>
> *Admission tutors feel under pressure to "get the numbers right", a pressure that has increased now that there are financial penalties for not meeting recruitment targets. They are also likely to be blamed when drop-out rates are linked to admitting "the wrong students" ' (Payne and Storan, 1995: 14, 17).*

> *'Course prospectuses and advertising are unlikely to become more realistic while institutions remain under pressure to recruit extra students' (Kember, 1995: 211).*

As outlined in Chapter 11, the fact that the higher education sector has expanded without extra resources has meant that many institutions have tried to accommodate a larger number of students without expanding or improving existing services. Speaking on the BBC 2 programme *The Knowledge* (17 October 1995), Stephen McNair, Associate Director of NIACE, pointed out that while the expansion of higher education and policies on wider access have brought into the system people whose background is very different from that of previous students, the support services are not in place to assist their progress:

> *'Many institutions have simply grown rather than transformed themselves. Some which worked well with small numbers don't work well with large numbers.'*

Some have suggested that the easiest way to improve retention would be to recruit only from groups perceived as 'safe' and low risk: i.e. those with good conventional examination grades. For example, the Audit Commission (1993) argues that the apparent correlation between prior GCSE results and non-completion in further education indicates that the application of more exacting entrance conditions may help to solve the problem – along with better teaching and on-course counselling:

> *'In particular the evidence implies that students with modest GCSE results ... should not be admitted to A-level courses without being made aware of their low chances of success.'*

Some researchers have expressed fears that the tying of funding to completion rates could lead to greater screening of applicants, with students with no, or non-standard, qualifications being seen as a liability:

> *'The temptation of any institutions seeking growth or survival in the new further education market place is likely to be to increase the market share of "safe", low cost, high-unit earning students. Although institutions are encouraged not to tie resourcing to unit earning, it is natural to look at units gained against related expenditure as one of the first steps in determining cost-effectiveness. The average or even better than average student becomes the benchmark of what is affordable to provide for whom' (Mansell and Parkin, 1990: 19).*

> *'The use of non-completion rates as a performance indicator can imply tacit or unwitting support for illiberal and restrictive entry policies. As a general performance indicator, non-completion is a blunt instrument that is likely to encourage some undesirable practices' (Bourner et al., 1991).*

Consolidation of student numbers in higher education has also generated anxiety that the number of 'non-standard' students accepted might be reduced if they were believed to have a higher than average risk of dropping out:

> *'Consolidation of the HE system may have a disproportionate impact on adult learners, particularly in institutions which choose to return to their traditional roles and clientele. There is a danger that traditional notions of HE linked with crude performance indicators will encourage institutions to do this, competing with each other to recruit less qualified young people rather than older learners, although the latter may achieve better results' (McNair, 1993).*

An investigation into the impact of consolidation on opportunities for 'non-standard' applicants concluded that new universities were unlikely to renege on their commitment to non-standard students on academic grounds but that old universities might be more selective about the students they admit. However, it was found that in most cases:

> *'non-standard entry was so embedded in institutional missions, in the balance of supply-and-demand at departmental and course level, and in the professional value systems of most staff members – that no retreat was likely' (Bargh, Scott and Smith, 1994).*

Moreover, this research literature shows that mature and other so-called 'non-standard' students are not, *per se*, a 'high risk' group although they are sometimes regarded as such in more conservative institutions. The maintenance of a cultural divide between the old and new universities – the former more traditional and elite, based largely on full-time attendance; the latter more committed to open entry and flexibility – has led to different perceptions of mature students. According to Bargh, Scott and Smith (1994), they are regarded in old universities as motivated but of average academic ability, whereas in new universities they are considered as some of the best students: 'There their presence is seen as a catalyst for innovation in teaching, learning, assessment and student care.'

Despite some survey findings that mature students are more likely than those of standard age to leave courses early, some of the institutional evidence available indicates that they are less likely than younger ones to discontinue programmes of study. Moreover, their performance is as good as, if not better than that of other students in many subjects. Although some have personal problems that are beyond the control or influence of the institution, these are often linked to an underlying dissatisfaction with the learning experience, which, if picked up sufficiently early, could be dealt with before a decision is made to withdraw. The available evidence indicates that students' motivation and the quality of the institutional support they receive have a greater impact on their progress than qualifications on entry.

Nevertheless, there will always be some who, for one reason or another, are obliged to interrupt or terminate their studies. As one report has commented, admitting mature students exposes institutions to the 'predictable crises of adult life which can prevent even the best motivated and prepared student from completing a course' (Payne and Storan, 1995). Thus Robertson (1994) argues for greater use of interim awards which would allow people to exit temporarily or permanently with a credit or credits which would have currency in the labour market or enable them to move to another institution at a later date.

Dealing with Non-Completion

Mansell and Parkin (1990) have advised institutions against undertaking further research into the causes of withdrawal, arguing that a number of studies have already been conducted and that the reasons vary from individual to individual. They also argue that locally-based research could be an excuse for avoiding action.

Despite the diversity of institutions, students and courses, there are, as Chapter 8 has indicated, a number of common factors involved in mature student withdrawal and institutions can take account of these without necessarily conducting further research. However, Mansell and Parkin's proposal ignores the crucial importance of institutional enquiries into non-completion in order to identify service deficiencies and possible intervention strategies. If a course or department is losing over 50 per cent of its students, then there is obviously something seriously wrong that merits investigation. As demonstrated by the study at Sheffield Hallam University (Moore, 1995), telephone or face-to-face interviews with former students can yield important insights into why they have left the institution or specific courses. Such information may suggest appropriate prevention strategies in the form of new initiatives and improvements in existing procedures and services.

Regular monitoring of student experience, progress and satisfaction is a valuable prevention strategy. This requires close staff–student contacts, good guidance and counselling services and, where possible, a personal tutor system. Another helpful strategy, adopted by several of the institutions that responded to this project, would be the appointment of an officer with special responsibility for monitoring retention rates who could disseminate guidelines on withdrawal to staff and students, identify the major factors involved in student withdrawals and propose institutional strategies to combat them.

Exchanges between comparable institutions on their experience of student loss and the implementation of any successful strategies for counteracting it would also be useful.

There is no doubt that support strategies introduced to improve retention may be costly. However, unless there is action, at a national level, on the issue of student financial support, non-completion rates must inevitably rise. They will also continue to rise unless institutions implement some of the other personal and academic measures to support students outlined in the previous chapters. While the further education sector can call on Additional Learning Support Units provided by the FEFC, many institutions are finding it difficult to fund areas such as tutorial time and study skills that are not eligible for central funding support. Running courses and keeping libraries open outside normal working hours, providing continuous pastoral support such as guidance and counselling, operating telephone helplines and providing practical support such as childcare facilities, are all expensive and difficult to provide, especially now that both sectors are facing substantial cuts in central funding over the next three years. If institutions do not or cannot provide these forms of support, however, the loss of substantial numbers of students may, in the long run, prove far more costly.

Bibliography

Abramson, M. (1994) 'Franchising, access, quality and exclusivity: some observations from recent research into further and higher education partnerships', *Journal of Access Studies*, 9 (1), 109–114.

Ainley, P. (1994) *Degrees of Difference: Higher education in the 1990s*, Lawrence and Wishart.

Audit Commission and Her Majesty's Inspectorate (1993) *Unfinished Business: Full-time educational courses for 16–19-year-olds*, HMSO.

Bargh, C., Scott, P. and Smith, D. (1994) 'Access and Consolidation: The impact of reduced student intakes on opportunities for non-standard applicants', Centre for Policy Studies in Education, University of Leeds.

Barnett, R. (1987) 'Part-time degree courses: institutional provision in the UK', *Higher Education Review*, 19 (3), 7–25.

Beddow, A. (1994) 'A Pilot Evaluation of the Adult Evening Curriculum', Exeter Tertiary College.

Benn, R. (1994) 'Factors Affecting Withdrawals in Higher Education', a paper presented at a conference on Comparative Issues in Access to Higher Education, Maine, 22–25 June.

Bird, J., Crawley, G. and Sheibani, A. (1993) *Franchising and Access to Higher Education: A study of HE/FE collaboration*, Department of Employment.

Booth, J., Layer, G. and Moore, R. (1994) 'Access, credit and guidance: the CNAA/UDACE Guidance in Higher Education Project', *Journal of Access Studies*, 9 (1), 146–153.

Bord, M. (1988) *Able to Manage: A national survey of the progress and performance of part-time Diploma in Management Studies students*, CNAA Development Series, 12.

Boshier, R. (1973) 'Educational participation and dropout: a theoretical model', *Adult Education* (US), XXIII (4), 225–282.

Bourner, T. and Barlow, J. (1991) *The Student Induction Handbook: Practical activities for institutions and new students*, Kogan Page.

—— and Hamed, M. (1987a) 'Degree awards in the public sector of higher education: comparative results for A-level and non A-level entrants', *Journal of Access Studies*, 2 (1), 25–41.

——, —— (1987b) *Entry Qualifications and Degree Performance*, CNAA.

Bourner, T., Reynolds, A., Hamed, M. and Barnett, R. (1991) *Part-Time Students and Their Experience of Higher Education*, Society for Research into Higher Education and Open University Press.

Brady, D. and Metcalfe, A. (1994) 'Staff and student perceptions of franchising', *Journal of Access Studies*, 9 (2), 271–277.

Brady, M. (1993) 'An evaluation of an access mathematics programme', *Journal of Access Studies*, 8 (2), 237–245.

Britton, C. and Baxter, A. (1994) 'Mature student routes into higher education', *Journal of Access Studies*, 9 (2), 215–228.

Brown, A. and Brimrose, J. (1992) 'Skills and Qualifications Required for Entry into Higher Education in England: Current practice and future policy', University of Surrey, Department of Educational Studies.

Bryant, R. and Noble, M. (1989) 'Grants, debts and second-chance students', *Adult Education*, 61 (4), 326–341.

Capizzi, E. (1994) 'Collecting data on students: new systems, new opportunities and more problems', *Journal of Access Studies*, 9 (2), 288–296.

Carlton, E. (1994) 'Counsellors face crack-up', *Times Higher Education Supplement*, 14 January.

Clare, J. (1995) 'Universities fail to make the grade', *Daily Telegraph*, 22 March.

Clarke, J. (1989) 'This is a Lifetime Thing: Outcomes for basic education students from Hackney AEI and the Hackney Reading Centre', ALFA and North and East London Open College Network.

Council for National Academic Awards (1990) *Some Factors Associated with Honours Degree Performance: An exploratory study using the CNAA student database*, CNAA.

—— (1992) *Progression and Performance in Higher Education*, CNAA.

Cullen, M-A. (1994) *Weighing It Up: A case study of discontinuing access students*, University of Edinburgh, Centre for Continuing Education, Occasional Paper Series No. 2.

Daniels, S. (1990) *Deaf Students in Higher Education: A survey of policy and practice*, RNID.

Davies, P. (1994) 'Fourteen years on, what do we know about Access students? Some reflections on national statistical data', *Journal of Access Studies*, 9 (1), 44–60.

—— (1995) 'Response or resistance? Access students and government policies on admissions', *Journal of Access Studies*, 10 (1), 72–80.

—— and Yates, J. (1987) 'The progress of former access students in higher education', *Journal of Access Studies*, 2 (1), 7–24.

Dekker, A. and Whitfield, R. (1989) *Completion Rates and Other Performance Indicators in Educational Opportunities for Unwaged Adults*, NIACE REPLAN.

Department for Education (1995) *The Government's Expenditure Plans 1995–96, 1997–98*, OFSTED.

Department of Education and Science (1992) 'Leaving Rates among First Year Degree Students in English Polytechnics and Colleges', *Statistical Bulletin 9/92*, DES.

—— *Statistical Bulletin 18/92*, DES.

—— *1993 Departmental Report*, February, CM 2210.

Duke, F. (1987) 'Degrees of experience: are the needs and expectations of mature adults and school leavers compatible?', *Journal of Access Studies*, 2 (1), 54–63.

Edwards, R. (1993) *Mature Women Students: Separating or connecting family and education*, Taylor and Francis.

Finn, D. (1995) 'Studying while unemployed', *Adults Learning*, 6 (9), 272–274.

Foong Lee, M., Regan, L., Sims, L., Uche, R.Z. and Woodrow, M. (1994) 'Accelerated and Intensive Routes to Higher Education', Second Annual Report of the Research and Evaluation Project, University of North London.

Further Education Development Agency (1995) *Supporting Part-Time Learners*, FEDA.

Further Education Funding Council (1995) *Chief Inspector's Annual Report, 1994–5*, FEFCE.

Further Education Unit (1987) *Access to Further and Higher Education. A discussion document*, FEU.

—— (1993) *Training Credits: Implications for colleges*, FEU.

—— (1994) 'Staying on or dropping out?', *Newsletter*, April, 8–9.

Glynn, D.R. and Jones, H.A. (1967) 'Student wastage', *Adult Education*, 10 (3).

Green, M. and Percy, K. (1991) 'Gender and access', in Chotty, C. (ed.) *Post-16 Education: Studies in access and achievement*, Kogan Page.

Hamblin, P.J. (1990) 'Attendance Patterns and Reasons for Drop Out in Adult Non-Vocational Classes', dissertation submitted in part requirement for the MEd degree of the University of Sheffield.

Hand, A., Gambles, J. and Cooper, E. (1994) 'Individual Commitment to Learning: Individuals' decision-making about "lifetime learning"', *Employment Department Research Series*, No. 42, Employment Department.

Harvey, C. (1995a) 'An Examination of Non-Completion Rates of Students on Stage 1 of FAETC at Norton Radstock College and the Reasons for Non-Completion', paper for Postgraduate Certificate in Education (FE), A367 Researching Practice in Continuing Education, University of the West of England.

Harvey, C. (1995b) 'Increasing course completion rates', *Adults Learning*, 6 (6), 178–179.

Her Majesty's Inspectorate (1991a) *Higher Education in Further Education Colleges: Franchising and other forms of collaboration. HMI Report 228/9/NS*, HMSO

—— (1991b) *Student Completion Rates in Further Education. HMI Report 26/91/NS*, HMSO.

—— (1993) 'Higher Education in the Polytechnics and Colleges: Student support services in higher education', *Education Observed Series*, DfE.

Herrick, J.R. (1986) 'A Study of the Scale and the Reasons for Student Drop-Out from Non-Vocational Adult Education Classes Provided by the Northamptonshire Adult Education Service', dissertation submitted in part requirement for the MEd degree of the University of Sheffield.

Hibbett, A. (1986) 'Dropping out or staying on: characteristics of dropout students and course completers', *Studies in the Education of Adults*, 18 (2), 71–81.

Higher Education Funding Council (England) (1995) *Funding the Relationship: Report on the relationship between higher education and further education*, HEFCE.

Higher Education Quality Council (1994) *Guidance and Counselling in Higher Education*, HEQC.

Johnes, J. (1990) 'Determinants of student wastage in higher education', *Studies in Higher Education*, 15 (1), 87–100.

Johnston, R. and Bailey, R. (1984) *Mature Students: Perceptions and experiences of full-time and part-time higher education*, Sheffield City Polytechnic, Department of Applied Social Sciences.

Karkalas, A. and MacKenzie, A. (1995) 'Travelling hopefully: Access and post-Access experience of adults who do not proceed to higher education', *Journal of Access Studies*, 10 (1). 20–39.

Kember, D. (1995) *Open Learning Courses for Adults: A model of student progress*, Englewood Cliffs, New Jersey: Education Technology Publications.

Kensington and Chelsea College (1995) Reports arising from surveys of full-time and part-time students (unpublished).

Kubie, L.S. (1966) 'The ontogeny of the dropout problem', in Pervin, L. *et al.* (eds) *College Dropout and the Utilisation of Talent*, Princeton University Press.

Labour Party (1990) *Opportunities for Students with Disabilities: Survey and consultative proposals for improving access to higher education for students with disabilities. A survey of universities and polytechnics*, Labour Party.

Leach, R. and Webb, W. (1992) 'Opportunities through open learning', in Calder, J. (ed.) *Disaffection and Diversity: Overcoming the barriers for adult learners*, Falmer Press, 91–109.

Lee, M. (1991) 'Culture shock', *Education*, 18 October.

Liverpool John Moores University (1993) 'Analysis of the Pattern, Incidence and Extent of Student Withdrawals in 1990–91 and 1991–92. Report submitted to the Operations Board', LJMU.

—— (1995a) 'Analysis of Retention Rates and Success Rates for the 1990 Cohort of Full-Time Degree Students', LJMU.

—— (1995b) 'Report on the Reasons given by Students for Withdrawing from LJMU Award Programmes', LJMU.

Lucas, S. and Ward, K. (1985) 'Mature students at Lancaster University', *Adult Education*, 58 (2), 151–157.

McIntosh, N.E. (1975) 'Open admission: an open or revolving door?', *Universities Quarterly*, Spring.

——, Woodley, A. and Morrison, V. (1980) 'Student demand and progression at the Open University', *Distance Education*, 1 (1), 37–60.

McKenna, M. (1988) 'Shaping change: the need for a new paradigm in higher education', *Adult Education* (US), 5 (10), 4.

McKeown, B. *et al.* (1993) 'The student point of view in attrition research', *Canadian Journal of Higher Education*, 23 (2), 65–85.

McNair, S. (1993) *An Adult Higher Education: A vision. A policy discussion paper*, NIACE.

—— (1995) 'Paying for an adult higher education', *Adults Learning*, 6 (9), 278–279.

McPherson, A. and Paterson, L. (1990) 'Findings from first year entry in universities and polytechnics and colleges of higher education in the Scottish public sector', *Higher Education*, 19.

Mansell, P. and Parkin, C. (1990) 'Student Drop Out: A handbook for managers.' Unpublished report from FEU project RP539, 'Student Participation and Wastage: From Research to Practice', FEU.

Mason, R. (1989) 'Adults and science: new prospects and perennial problems', *Adults Learning*, 1 (2), 37–39.

Maynard, E.M. and Pearsall, S.J. (1994) 'What about male mature students? A comparison of the experiences of men and women students', *Journal of Access Studies*, 9 (2), 229–240.

Metcalf, H. (1993) *Non-traditional Students' Experience of Higher Education: A review of the literature*, Committee of Vice Chancellors and Principals.

Metcalfe, J.A. and Halstead, A. (1994) 'Open learning, drop-out and accreditation', *Adults Learning*, 5 (10), 261–263.

Moore, R. (1995) 'Retention Rates Research Project. Final report', Division of Access and Guidance, Sheffield Hallam University.

Munn, P., MacDonald, C. and Lowden, K. (1992) *Helping Adult Students Cope*, Scottish Council for Research in Education.

Nash, I. (1994) 'Adults find doors closed to learning', *Times Educational Supplement*, 9 September.

National Extension College (1991) *Who are the NEC's Invisible Students? A report of a student profile 1989/90*, NEC.

NIACE (1994) *What Price the Learning Society? Results of the MORI poll survey*, NIACE.

—— (1995) *Adult Learners in Further Education Colleges*, NIACE.

NIAE (1970) *Adequacy of Provision*, NIAE.

Open University, West Midlands Region (1995) 'Towards an Understanding of Part-Time Student Non-Completion', Open University, West Midlands Region.

Parry, G. (1986) 'From patronage to partnership', *Journal of Access Studies*, 1 (1), 45–53.

Payne, J. (1995) 'Qualifications Between 16 and 18: A comparison of achievements on routes beyond compulsory schooling', *Employment Department Research Series*, Youth Cohort Report No. 32.

—— and Storan, J. (1995) 'Further and Higher Education Progression Project', Final Report, Division of Continuing Education, South Bank University.

Pennell, H. and Varlaam, A. (1993) 'Access to Higher Education and Profile of Access Students in London', Centre for Educational Research, London School of Economics.

Polytechnic of North London (1991) 'Making HE Work for People with Disabilities', Disability Working Group Report for PNL's Advisory Group.

Pritchard, S. (1995) 'Dropping out: it may be the smartest move', *Independent*, 19 October.

Pupynin, K. and Crowder, M. (1995) 'Individual Commitment to Learning. Understanding learner motivation: An overview', Individual Commitment Branch, Employment Department, Research Series.

PUSH (1994) *PUSH Guide to Which University 1995*.

Redpath, B. and Robus, N. (1989) *Mature Students' Incomings and Outgoings*, HMSO.

Rickwood, P.W. (1993) 'The Experience of Transfer: A study of a cohort of students who used Open University credits to transfer to other institutions of higher education', Open University, West Midlands Region.

Robbins, Lord (1963) *Report of the Committee on Higher Education* [The Robbins Report], HMSO.

Roberts, D. and Higgins, T. (1992) *Higher Education: The student experience*, HEIST.

Roberts, G. and Webb, W. (1979) 'Drop out in adult education', *Educational Research*, 22 (1).

Robertson, D. (1994) *Choosing to Change: Extending access, choice and mobility in higher education.* The report of the HEQC CAT Development Project, HEQC.

—— (1995) 'Funding the learning society', *Adults Learning*, 6 (9), 275–277.

Roderick, G. (1981) 'Mature Students in Further and Higher Education', University of Sheffield, Division of Continuing Education.

—— and Bell, J.M. (1981) 'Unqualified mature students at the University of Sheffield', *Studies in Higher Education*, 6 (2), 123–129.

——, —— and Hamilton, S. (1982) 'Unqualified mature students in British universities', *Studies in Adult Education*, 6 (2), 123–129.

Rogers, J. (1971) *Adults Learning*, Open University Press.

Sanders, C. (1995a) 'Second best degree risk', *Times Higher Education Supplement*, 28 April.

—— (1995b) 'Poor students rush for advice', *Times Higher Education Supplement*, 22 September.

Sanders, J. (1977) 'Students Said: A report on the experiences of 48 adult literacy students', Manchester Adult Literacy Research Project.

Singh, R. (1990) 'Ethnic minority experience in higher education', *Higher Education Quarterly*, 44 (4), 344–359.

Smith, D. and Saunders, M. (1988) 'Part-time higher education prospects and practices', *Higher Education Review*, 20 (3), 7–26.

——, —— (1991) *Other Routes: Part-time higher education policy*, Society for Research into Higher Education.

Smith, G. and Bailey, V. (1993) *Staying the Course*, BTEC.

Smith, R.N. (1979) 'Student awareness of attendance problems: a survey of drop outs', *Adult Education*, 52, 107–110.

Smithers, A. and Griffin, A. (1986) 'Mature students at university: entry experience and outcomes', *Studies in Higher Education*, 11 (3), 257–268.

Stott, C. (1994) 'Securing wider access', *Journal of Access Studies*, 9 (1), 124–130.

Taylor, J. and Johnes, J. (1989) 'Undergraduate non-completion rates: differences between universities', *Higher Education*, 18 (2), 209–225.

——, —— (1991) 'Non-completion of a degre course and its effect on the subsequent experience of non-completers in the labour market', *Studies in Higher Education*, 16 (1), 73–81.

Temple, J. (1991) 'Age of Opportunity? Progression routes and outcomes for students in adult basic education from Hackney AEI and Hackney Reading Centre', ALFA.

Tight, M. (1987) 'Access and part-time undergraduate study', *Journal of Access Studies*, 2 (1), 12–20.

—— (1991) *Higher Education: A part-time perspective*, Society for Research into Higher Education and Open University Press.

Tinto, V. (1975) 'Dropout from higher education: a theoretical synthesis of recent research', *Review of Education Research*, 45, 89–125.

Uden, T. (1994) *The Will to Learn: Individual commitment and adult learning. A policy discussion paper*, NIACE.

Underwood, J.G. (1974) 'Adult students: reasons for coming and going', *Adult Education*, 46, 343–345.

University of Brighton (1994) 'Access Students in Southern Access Higher Education Institutions: Research summary', University of Brighton, Equal Opportunities Committee.

University of Edinburgh (1995) 'Helping Students with Study Skills: An integrated computer-based package for staff and students. An overview', University of Edinburgh, Centre for Research in Learning and Instruction.

Utley, A. (1994a) 'Drop-outs skew FE Targets', *Times Higher Education Supplement*, 14 January.

—— (1994b) 'Pain and loneliness of the first-year student', *Times Higher Education Supplement*, 30 December.

—— (1995a) 'Participation down … A-level grades up', *Times Higher Education Supplement*, 18 August.

—— (1995b) 'Colleges have to pay back money', *Times Higher Education Supplement*, 20 October.

Vinegrad, M. (1980) 'A profile of part-time, adult degree students', *Studies in Adult Education*, 12, 147–154.

Wagner, L. (1990) 'The economics of wider participation', in Parry, G. and Wake, C. (eds) *Access and Alternative Futures for Higher Education*, Hodder and Stoughton, 43–60.

Wakeford, N. (1994) 'Becoming a mature student: the social risks of identification', *Journal of Access Studies*, 9 (2), 241–256.

Walker, P. (1975) 'The university performance of mature students', *Research in Education*, 14, 1–13.

Webb, S., Davies, P., Green, P., Thompson, A. and Williams, J., with Weller P., Lovell, T. and Shah, S. (1994) *Alternative Entry to Higher Education. Summary report*, Employment Department and FEU.

——, ——, Williams, J. and Green, P. (1994) 'Alternative and access entrants to higher education: tracks, triggers and choices', *Journal of Access Studies*, 9 (2), 197–214.

Weil, S.W. (1986) 'Non-traditional learners within the traditional higher education institutions: discovery and disappointment', *Studies in Higher Education*, 11, 219–235.

Whittaker, A. (1994) 'Where Do They Go and Why? Student drop-out in adult education', City and Islington College.

Wilkinson, G. (1982) 'Student dropout', *Adult Education*, 55, 32–37.

Williams, J., Cocking, J. and Davies, L. (1989) *Words or Deeds*, Council for Racial Equality.

Wirral Metropolitan College (1993) 'Financial Barriers to Further and Higher Education for Adult Students', project report.

—— (1994) Student Retention Report No. 4: 1993/94.

Woodley, A. (1987) 'Understanding adult student drop-out', in Thorpe, M. and Grugeon, D. (eds) *Open Learning for Adults*, Longman, 110–124.

—— (1987) 'Has the Open University been an unqualified success?', *Journal of Access Studies*, 2, 7–14.

—— (1984) 'The older the better: a study of mature student performance in British universities', *Research in Education*, 32, 32–50.

—— (1992) 'Disaffection and distance education', in Calder, J. (ed.) *Disaffection and Diversity: Overcoming the barriers for adult learners*, Falmer Press, 110–124.

—— and Parlett, M. (1983) 'Student drop-out', *Teaching at a Distance*, 24, 2–23.

——, Wagner, L., Slowey, M., Hamilton, M. and Fulton, O. (1987) *Choosing to Learn: Adults in education*, Open University Press.

Yates, J. and Davies, P. (1986) 'The Progress and Performance of Former Access Students in Higher Education 1984–1986', Final Report, Roehampton Institute.

YHAFHE (1993) *Gender Network Newsletter*, 29 January.

Young, S. (1994) 'Degree dropout rate rises', *Times Educational Supplement*, 19 August.

Newspapers and journals

Daily Telegraph: 22 March 1995

Education: 8 July 1994, 18 October 1991, 17 March 1995

Financial Times: 8 December 1993

Guardian: 12 November 1994

TEC Guidance Update: March 1993.

Times Higher Education Supplement: 14 January 1994, 30 December 1994, 20 January 1995, 7 March 1995, 21 April 1995, 20 October 1995, 24 November 1995, 1, 8, 22, 29 December 1995

Appendices

Appendix 1: Questionnaire Used in Institutional Survey

An investigation of the retention, non-completion and withdrawal patterns of mature students on accredited and award courses in further and higher education conducted by NIACE for the Employment Department.

Name of institution/organisation:

Name of contact person:

1. What system is used to collect and record student data?

2. What information on student non-completion/withdrawal is currently recorded on central or computerised management systems?

3. What parts of the institution have responsibility for collecting and recording such data?

4. For what purpose(s) is data on student non-completion/withdrawal collected?

5. How is student withdrawal defined? (What and whose criteria are used?)

6. What methods and cut-off points are used to calculate non-completion rates?

7. How are reasons for withdrawal categorised?

8. What procedures are in place to contact students who have withdrawn from a course or who have failed to attend for a significant period?

9. What measures have been put in place to increase student retention?

10. To what extent is evidence of student withdrawal used in programme or institutional review or staff appraisal?

11. Additional information/comments

We would be grateful if you could supply, for this study, any data on home student non-completion/withdrawal since 1991, disaggregated (if such detail is available) by:

(a)   subject/qualification level

(b)   year of course

(c)   entry route/qualification on entry

(d)   mode of attendance

(e)   age

(f)   gender

(g)   ethnic origin

(h)   method of funding (e.g. mandatory or discretionary award; employer-funded; self-funded)

(i)   reasons for withdrawal/non-completion

Please note: The name of your institution will not be used in any report if you prefer this information to be kept confidential.

Thank you for your kind co-operation.

Appendix 2: Leaver Codes

Please tick the one box which describes the main reasons for this learner leaving the course.

Class-related reasons

Enrolled but never attended _____ ☐
Enrolled to this class in error _____ ☐
Left class _____ ☐

Job-related reasons

Started job _____ ☐
Changed job _____ ☐
Started government scheme (YT/ET) _____ ☐
Other job-related issues _____ ☐

Course-related reasons

Unsuccessful in exams _____ ☐
Chose different course _____ ☐
Learner changed their plans _____ ☐
Misunderstood/misinformed about nature of course ___☐
Course was too difficult _____ ☐
Course was too easy _____ ☐
Disliked course _____ ☐
Disliked teaching staff _____ ☐
Completed work on topics wanted _____ ☐
Finished course (roll on/roll off) _____ ☐
Other course-related reasons _____ ☐

College-related reasons

Inadequate general facilities, e.g. library,
refectory, toilets, social areas _____ ☐
Inadequate specialist facilities,
e.g. computers, machinery, equipment, etc. _____ ☐
Other college-related reasons _____ ☐

Personal reasons

Moved from area _____ ☐
Illness _____ ☐
Family/personal reasons _____ ☐
Financial reasons _____ ☐
Took too much on _____ ☐
Travel difficulties _____ ☐
Other personal reasons _____ ☐

Appendix 3: Transition into Higher Education Questionnaire

(University of Bradford Access Unit)

Entering higher education is like entering another world; a world that can be both stimulating and exciting, and sometimes confusing and terrifying. The culture and language are often alien to new students and though students do adjust to higher education once they are part of it, it can be an unnecessarily painful experience.

This questionnaire is designed to raise some issues relevant to being a student in higher education so they can be discussed and clarified before you start your course. Thinking through your expectations of higher education and matching this with what is likely to be involved is sound preparation for a successful student life.

Have a go at answering the following questions. It is not a test and it doesn't matter if you don't know the answer or have to guess – all will be revealed in due course!

1. What is a mature student?

2. What is an undergraduate student?

3. What is the age range of students on degree courses?

4. What do the following stand for?

    BA

    BEd

    BEng

    BPharm

    BSc

5. What are the different classifications that can be awarded?

6. What is an LEA?

7. Are mandatory grants means tested?

8. What is the grant award meant to cover?

9. Can you get more money in your grant if you have been in paid employment?

10. When can you apply for a student loan?

11. Can you apply for more than one student loan in one year?

12. Does money from the Access Fund have to be paid back?

13. What is a lecture?

14. What is a seminar?

15. What is a group tutorial?

16. What is the role of a personal tutor?

17. What is a semester?

18. What is an academic year?

19. What is a module?

20. How are students assessed?

21. Are lecturers assessed?

22. What do tutors award marks for when they mark essays?

23. What is plagiarism?

24. What are the consequences of plagiarism?

25. What is the purpose of an examination?

26. Name two revision activities that would help you prepare effectively for an examination.

27. How are lecturers assessed?

28. What support services do universities provide for students?

29. What special perks or benefits are available to students?

30. Are these services and benefits also available to part-time students?

Index